KOREAN LANGUAGE
for Beginners

Korean Language for Beginners

Published in 2016 by Seoul Selection U.S.A., Inc.
4199 Campus Drive, Suite 550, Irvine, CA 92612

Phone: 949-509-6584 / Seoul office: 82-2-734-9567
Fax: 949-509-6599 / Seoul office: 82-2-734-9562
Email: publisher@seoulselection.com

ISBN: 978-1-62412-068-8
Library of Congress Control Number: 2016940828

Printed in the Republic of Korea

Originally published by Cafoscarina Edizioni, Venice (2014)

Andrea De Benedittis

KOREAN LANGUAGE
for Beginners

In collaboration with Giuseppina De Nicola and Lee Sang Suk

Seoul Selection

Contents

Author's Note

S tudying a new language is, without doubt, a challenging task, but at the same time, it is the most effective tool in our human hands to bring about peace in the world. It enables us to take a look inside other cultures and civilizations, get to know people from different backgrounds, and understand others and ourselves a little more deeply.

Studying the Korean language is even more challenging and fascinating than studying other languages. Korea has an ancient culture. Over the centuries, it has—amazingly—been able to mix all the influences coming from Central Asia, the Steppes, Manchuria, China, Japan, and the West into a beautiful, brilliant, and unique new culture. This cultural richness has affected the Korean language, following a very long process of adoption and establishment of new terms, sounds, and expressions coming from abroad. And even if the vocabulary of the language is already boundless, new generations of Koreans continue to create and add new words (neologisms) day by day. In this way, they update their language to reflect new trends and new social phenomena. It is difficult to find another language in the world that is as creative and innovative as Korean.

However, this makes Korean a very difficult language to learn, above all for people whose mother language is neither Chinese nor Japanese. It takes years to become fluent and pronounce the language well enough to be understood. But don't be discouraged. After a few weeks of study, you will start to recognize words, make sentences, and have simple (but miraculous) conversations with other Korean speakers! (At the very beginning, it will be quite humiliating, but this is part of the game we decided to play.) Understanding the words to Korean songs, dramas, and movies will be the next step.

This book is a complete guide for people who want to learn the language, starting from the very beginning, and learn the alphabet and the correct sounds of vowels, consonants, and diphthongs. It was written for people who want an easy but systematic approach to the language. The writer is a non-native speaker (me!) who started learning the language from ZERO, just like you and spent years in Korea trying to reach a better level of proficiency.

Don't forget. The language you are going to study using this book, the people who speak it, and the culture that produced it are AMAZING. It is important that you remember that while studying this language. By reading the pages of the book, working through the exercises, and memorizing the words step by step, you will be forging your keys to the doors of Korean culture.

Andrea De Benedittis
From a messy room in Venice, 2016

How to Use This Book

1. This book is divided into fourteen units. The first three deal with the Korean alphabet (vowels, consonants, and diphthongs), sounds, and phonology, and explain the main features of the language (verbs, linguistic protocol, particles, punctuation marks, and the lexicon).

2. Some simple grammatical elements will be introduced from Unit 4. Each unit has a cover page featuring the main words used in that unit. Unlike many other Korean textbooks, this one begins with the formal level of speech. We have chosen to begin this way because verbs follow a more regular conjugation pattern; therefore, it is easier for beginners to understand.

3. Every unit begins with a short text, which introduces and contextualizes the gramma points examined in that unit. Finally, each unit contains a section providing an in-depth analysis of the grammar points taught in that unit, as well as exercises for practice.

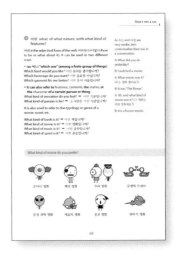

4. To download the MP3 files, go to http://www.seoulselection.com/bookstore and search for Korean Language for Beginners.

5. In the appendix you can find the solutions to all the exercises in the book, conjugation tables, more detailed explanations on the usage of the topic and subject particles, and a guide to writing emails in Korean.

6. The book flaps are useful, as they contain tables summarizing the main content throughout the book.

Symbols and abbreviations

 additional information

 listening track

expression to memorize

 note_ note: grammatical note

 difficult exception

 clarification

In this book, Korean words have been transliterated in accordance with the revised romanization of Korean.

Acknowledgments

 This book wouldn't have been possible without the constant help of relatives, friends, and colleagues. We owe a special thank you to Giuseppe Pappalardo for all the remarks on linguistic terms, to "Professors" Calvetti and Riotto for all their precious advice. Giuseppina De Nicola contributed to the revision of the original version and Lee Sang Suk to the proofreading and adaptation of the Korean content. She also wrote the section titled "How to write an email," and hers is the voice on the listening tracks. 감사합니다!

Main Characters (등장인물)

나
me

곰인형
teddy bear

세종대왕
Great King Sejong

양반탈
mask of a noble

친구
friend

어머니
mother

아버지
father

선인장
cactus

귀신
ghost

부네탈
mask of lady

돌하르방
stone grandpa

양반
noble

남자친구
boyfriend

여자친구
girlfriend

신부
bride

신랑
groom

눈사람
snowman

고릴라
gorilla

원앙
mandarin duck
or lovebird

광대
clown

Unit 1

한글 1
Korean alphabet 1

| Introduction
| Vowels
| Consonants 1

 1

ㅏ [a]	ㅛ [yo]	ㅁ [m]	네 yes	언니 elder sister
ㅓ [eo]	ㅠ [yu]	ㅅ [s]	마음 heart	엄마 mom
ㅗ [o]	ㅐ [ae]	ㅇ [ng]	매미 cicada	오이 cucumber
ㅜ [u]	ㅔ [e]	가구 furniture	몸 body	이 tooth
ㅡ [eu]	ㅒ [yae]	가시 thorn	사슴 deer	이마 forehead
ㅣ [i]	ㅖ [ye]	개 dog	소 cow	
ㅑ [ya]	ㄱ [g]	거미 spider	아이 baby	
ㅕ [yeo]	ㄴ [n]	게 crab	악어 crocodile	

Introduction

The Korean alphabet is a writing system created in 1443 and promulgated in 1446 during the reign of King Sejong, the fourth King of Joseon Dynasty (1392-1910). Originally considered "vulgar writing"(*eonmun*, 언문), it first began to be widely utilized and appreciated after Japanese colonization of the peninsula, when it became an instrument of self-determination against foreigners' rule over Korean territory. The Korean alphabet is currently used in South Korea, where it is called Hangeul (한글, the term in this book); in North Korea, where it is called *Joseongeul* (조선글); and also by overseas Korean communities, mostly in China and the United States. Under a project abandoned in 2012, South Korea sought to export the alphabet abroad to provide a writing system to linguistic minorities lacking a proper writing system.

Its structure

The Chinese writing system is considered logographic. Korean also uses Hanja and Japanese uses Kanji, which would both be considered logographic. Japanese Hiragana, Katakana and Hangeul are all phonographic but that Hangeul has the distinction of also being phono-characterized.

Initially, the alphabet had twenty-eight main letters, which over time have been reduced to twenty-four. Eight are considered basic sounds, and from these derive all the other consonants and vowels. We must first distinguish between:

1. the five basic consonants [ㄱ, ㄴ, ㅁ, ㅅ, ㅇ] from which derive the fourteen simple consonants,

2. three basic vowels [·, ㅣ, ㅡ] from which derive the first ten, simple, or iotized, vowels.

From the fourteen simple consonants (ㄱ, ㄴ, ㄷ, ㄹ, ㅁ, ㅂ, ㅅ, ㅇ, ㅈ, ㅊ, ㅋ, ㅌ, ㅍ, ㅎ) are derived in turn five double consonants (ㄲ, ㄸ, ㅃ, ㅆ, ㅉ) and eleven complex combinations (ㄳ, ㄵ, ㄶ, ㄺ, ㄻ, ㄼ, ㄽ, ㄾ, ㄿ, ㅀ, ㅄ). The ten simple vowels (ㅏ, ㅑ, ㅓ, ㅕ, ㅗ, ㅛ, ㅜ, ㅠ, ㅡ, ㅣ) are followed by four complex vowels (ㅐ, ㅒ, ㅔ, ㅖ) and seven diphthongs (ㅘ, ㅙ, ㅚ, ㅝ, ㅞ, ㅟ, ㅢ).

1 fourteen simple consonants

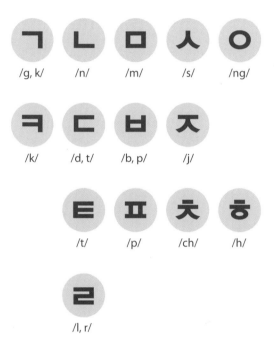

2 five double consonants

3 eleven complex combinations

4 ten simple vowels

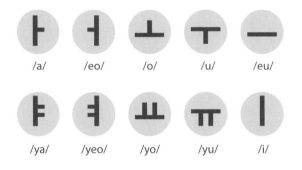

5 four complex vowels

6 seven diphthongs

Korean writing is conceived in blocks representing syllables, each composed of an initial consonant, a (medial) vowel or a diphthong, and finally an ending composed of one or two consonants known as batchim. Consider the following examples:

받침

Some pronunciation change if followed by this particle.
The word batchim (받침, literally meaning "basis, support") refers to consonants at the conclusion of a syllable. Not all syllable blocks have one; for instance, those in examples 1 and 2 don't have any. Example 3 has one, and example 4 has a double batchim.

How to write Korean syllables

Example 1

(C1 unvoiced +) V

Example 2

C1 + V

Example 3

C1 + V + C2

Example 4

C1 + V + C2 + C3

Vowels

The graphemes of Korean vowels are inspired by **three core elements** of Korean cosmology (heaven, man, earth), to which are respectively associated three graphic elements: a mark, a vertical line and a horizontal line.

| heaven | man | earth |

In addition to the sounds they represent, therefore, the single vowels also lend philosophical significance to the words that they form.

If we combine these three elements together, we obtain the vowels of the Korean alphabet. The sun (heaven) combined with man brings the graphic formation of the vowels ㅏ and ㅓ. The earth combined with the sun (heaven) brings the graphic formation of the vowels ㅗ and ㅜ.

If a vowel depicts a man standing in front of a rising sun (ㅏ), or a sun rising on the earth (ㅗ) this means the vowel has a positive nuance and is considered a positive or **solar vowel**.

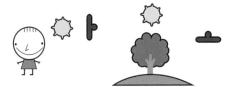

On the other hand, if the vowel depicts a man standing in front of a setting sun (ㅓ) or a sun under the earth (ㅜ), this implies a negative nuance, and the vowel is considered negative or lunar.

* Even if the vowels ㅣ and ㅡ are considered neutral, they behave as lunar vowels. So do the complex vowels ㅔ, ㅐ, ㅖ, ㅒ and ㅒ as these include the ㅓ vowel.

Examples

Negative nuance		Positive nuance	
덥다	[deopta]: to be hot	따뜻하다	[ttatteutada]: to be warm
더럽다	[deoreopta]: to be dirty	다랍다	[darapta]: to be lightly dirty
뚱뚱하다	[ttungttunghada]: to be fat	통통하다	[tongtonghada]: to be plump

Now let's try writing the first six vowels (a, eo, o, u, eu, i). Always pay attention to stroke order, which must be strictly respected when writing Korean.

Let's write!

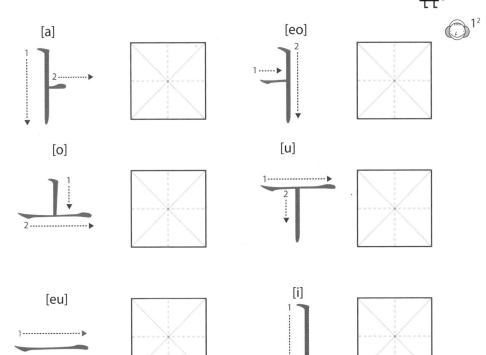

[a]

[eo]

[o]

[u]

[eu]

[i]

7

* When practicing the pronunciation of these vowels, pay attention to the next two points:

No vowel can be written alone in a syllabic block, but rather must always be accompanied by a consonant. When a syllable starts with a vowel, it must be preceded by the consonant ㅇ (ieung), which is unvoiced when it falls at the beginning of a syllable. That means that the vowels we have just learned are to be written like this:

① ㅓ is a broad "o". Open your mouth wide and then pronounce the sound. When pronouncing ㅗ, you half-close your mouth, like in the drawing.

아 (a), 어 (eo), 오 (o), 우 (u), 으 (eu), 이 (i)

Examples

오이 cucumber
아이 baby
이 tooth

② The ㅜ vowel corresponds the long "oo" sound found in "moon" and "too." On the contrary, ㅡ has no exact equivalent in English. It is similar to a short "oo" sound (as in "cook" and "book") but is pronounced without puckering the lips.

You must practice these two sounds, as a mispronunciation may change the meaning of a statement. Consider for example the verb kkuda (꾸다), which means "to dream" and which can easily be confused with the verb kkeuda (끄다), which means "to turn off".

If you mispronounce these sounds you may be misunderstood, as shown in the following examples:

Examples

검	[geom]: sword	곰	[gom]: bear
커피	[keopi]: coffee	코피	[kopi]: nosebleed
널다	[neolda]: to hang	놀다	[nolda]: to play, to idle away

If we add a "i" to these vowels, we obtain their **iotized** versions.

Let's write!

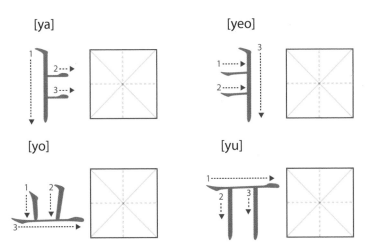

In addition to these vowels, there are also two types of "e". We can distinguish between a "closed" [e] (에) and a "broad" one æ(애), from which are derived their iotized versions (예, 얘).

Let's write

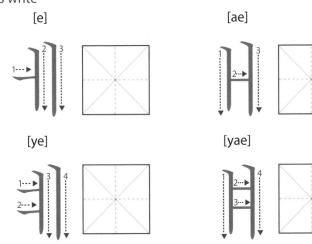

9

Vowels that sound similar ㅐ and ㅔ

In spoken Korean, there is actually little to no distinction between the pronunciation of these two vowels, except for those cases in which there is a risk of homophony.

Examples

개	[gae]: dog	게	[ge]: crab
모래	[morae]: sand	모레	[more]: the day after tomorrow
내	[nae]: my	네	[ne]: yes

Consonants

As mentioned above, there are five basic consonants in the Korean language. Each one graphically reproduce those parts of the phonatory system that facilitate the emission of that specific sound (lips, tongue, teeth, throat).

The ㄱ , 기역 ([giyeok]), corresponds to a voiceless or voiced velar occlusive, (e.g., 가, 구이, 아가, 악어)

The ㄴ , 니은 ([nieun]), corresponds to a nasal alveolar [n], (e.g., 나, 너, 네, 언니)

The ㅁ , 미음 ([mieum]), corresponds to a nasal bilabial [m], (e.g., 마, 엄마, 이마, 마음)

The ㅅ , 시옷 ([siot]) corresponds to a fricative alveolar [s], (e.g., 소, 이사, 어서)

* ㅅ followed by 이, or by an iotized vowel, is pronounced as a voiceless fricative post alveolar corresponding to the "sh" sound in English (e.g., 시, 쇼, 시기).

The ㅇ (이응, [ieung]) corresponds to a nasal velar. At the beginning of a syllable it is not pronounced, but if it is found in a batchim, it is pronounced a nasalized g— that is, the "ng" or ŋ sound. Voiceless examples include 엄마, 이마, and 마음; "ng" examples include 공간, 송어, and 멍멍이.

Let's write

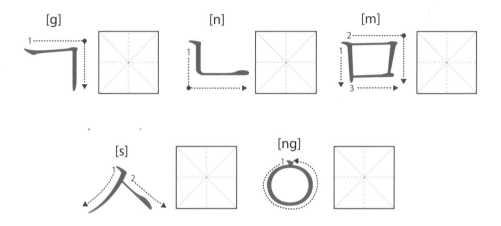

Now let's use these letters to write our first Korean words. When writing, the proportion of the syllables must be even, so in the beginning it can help to use paper with large squares.

Let's write

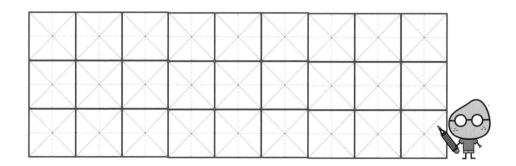

Write the following words in Korean.

게	crab		개	dog	
네	yes		이	tooth	
오이	cucumber		아이	baby	
엄마	mom		사슴	deer	
마음	heart		이마	forehead	
가구	furniture		가시	thorn	
소	cow		몸	body	
언니	elder sister		거미	spider	
매미	cicada		악어	crocodile	

Unit 2

한글 2
Korean alphabet 2

| Consonants 2
| Some features of Korean language

 2

ㄲ [kk]	ㅆ [ss]	굴 oyster	컴퓨터 computer
ㅋ [k]	ㅈ [j]	꿀 honey	탈 mask
ㄹ [r,l]	ㅉ [jj]	달 moon	토끼 rabbit
ㄷ [d]	ㅊ [ch]	딸 daughter	토마토 tomato
ㄸ [tt]	ㅎ [h]	말 horse	피아노 piano
ㅌ [t]	개구리 frog	물고기 fish	햄버거 hamburger
ㅂ [b]	거북이 turtle	사자 lion	휴대폰 cell phone
ㅃ [pp]	고양이 cat	새 bird	
ㅍ [p]	곰 bear	초콜릿 chocolate	

Consonants 2

By adding one or more strokes to the basic consonants we obtain others that can be grouped as follows.

From ㄱ we obtain ㄲ [kk] (or double ㄱ, romanized "kk") and ㅋ (ㄱ the "k" sound, an aspirated ㄱ)

When ㄱ, ㄲ, and ㅋ are followed by horizontal vowels such as ㅜ or ㅗ, the second stroke is written as a straight vertical line; whereas in front of vertical vowels such as ㅏ, ㅓ, ㅣ it is longer and curved.

고, 꼬, 코

거, 꺼, 커

Let's write

[kk]

[k]

Let's Try to
pronounce:
굴 = Oyster
꿀 = Honey
쿨 = Cool

Exercise 1   Pronounce the following syllables.

1) 가, 까, 카 - 거, 꺼, 커 - 고, 꼬, 코 - 구, 꾸, 쿠 - 기, 끼, 키

2) 고기, 고끼, 고키 - 아가, 아까, 아카 - 이기, 이끼, 이키

3) 아기, 아끼, 아키 - 여고, 여꼬, 여코 - 굴, 꿀, 쿨 - 길, 낄, 킬

4) 게, 께, 케 - 겔, 껠, 켈 - 갈, 깔, 칼 - 우기, 우끼, 우키

5) 아기니, 아끼니, 아키니 - 가고, 가꼬, 가코

From ㄴ we obtain ㄹ (the "r" and "l" sounds, alveolar liquid); ㄷ (the "d" sound, alveolar occlusive); ㄸ (or double ㄷ, romanized as "tt"); and ㅌ (the "t" sound, an aspirated ㄷ).

Let's write

[l, r]

[d]

[tt]

[t]

Exercise 2   Pronounce the following syllables.

1) 다, 따, 타 - 더, 떠, 터 - 도, 또, 토 - 두, 뚜, 투 - 디, 띠, 티

2) 고디, 고띠, 고티 - 아다, 아따, 아타 - 이디, 이띠, 이티

3) 어디, 어띠, 어티 - 여도, 여또, 여토 - 달, 딸, 탈 - 덜, 떨, 털

From ㅁ we obtain ㅂ (the "b" sound, bilabial occlusive); ㅃ (the double ㅂ sound, romanized as "pp"); and ㅍ (the "p" sound, an aspirated ㅂ).

Let's write

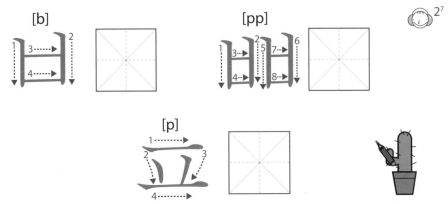

[b]

[pp]

[p]

Exercise 3 Pronounce the following syllables.

1) 바, 빠, 파 - 버, 뻐, 퍼 - 보, 뽀, 포 - 부, 뿌, 푸 - 비, 삐, 피

2) 고비, 고삐, 고피 - 오바, 오빠, 오파 - 이비, 이삐, 이피

3) 아비, 아삐, 아피 - 여보, 여뽀, 여포 - 불, 뿔, 풀 - 빌, 삘, 필

4) 베, 뻬, 페 - 벨, 뻴, 펠 - 발, 빨, 팔 - 우비, 우삐, 우피

From ㅅ we obtain ㅆ (a double ㅅ, romanized "ss"); ㅈ
(romanized "j," an alveo-palatal affricate sound); ㅉ (double ㅈ,
romanized "jj"); and ㅊ (a "ch" sound, or ㅈ with aspiration).

Let's write

[ss]

[j]

[jj]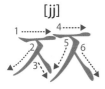

[ch]

Exercise 4   Pronounce the following syllables.

🐵2[10]

1) 사, 싸, 자, 차 - 서, 써, 저, 처 - 소, 쏘, 조, 초 - 수, 쑤, 주, 추

2) 고시, 고씨, 고지, 고치 - 아사, 아싸, 아자, 아차

3) 어서, 어써, 어저, 어처 - 살, 쌀, 잘, 찰 - 시, 씨, 지, 치

4) 사다, 싸다, 자다, 차다 - 셀, 쎌, 젤, 첼 - 설, 썰, 절, 철

5) 소다, 쏘다, 조다, 초다 - 이시, 이씨, 이지, 이치

Finally, from ㅇ we obtain ㅎ [h].

Let's write

🐵2[11]

[h]

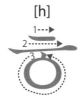

The ㅎ indicates an aspiration of the following vowel: the aspiration is **strong** when the ㅎ is at the beginning of a word, but it is **barely perceptible** when it is between two vowels or inside a word.

17

Exercise 5   Pronounce the following syllables.

2¹²

1) 한, 햄, 힘, 휴일, 휴가, 해고, 혀

2) 문화, 산하, 간호 , 변호사, 결혼, 올해, 변하다

* It is important to memorize the order of Korean letters, as this is
useful when searching for a word in a paper dictionary or in a list.
Order of Korean consonants: ㄱ (ㄲ) ㄴ ㄷ (ㄸ) ㄹ ㅁ ㅂ (ㅃ) ㅅ
(ㅆ) ㅇ ㅈ (ㅉ ㅊ ㅋ ㅌ ㅍ ㅎ).
Order of Korean vowels: ㅏ ㅐ ㅑ ㅒ ㅓ ㅔ ㅕ ㅖ ㅗ ㅘ ㅙ ㅚ ㅛ ㅜ
ㅝ ㅞ ㅟ ㅠ ㅡ ㅢ ㅣ.

Exercise 6   Put the following animals in alphabetical order.

물고기
☐ fish

사자
☐ lion

새
☐ bird

거북이
☐ turtle

개구리
☐ frog

고양이
☐ cat

말
☐ horse

곰
☐ bear

토끼
☐ rabbit

개
☐ dog

   In the first unit we learned the vowels and consonants
of the Korean language. In this unit, and the next we will
analyze some of the graphic and phonetic features of
these letters and of the Korean language. Before moving
on, let's first memorize the Korean names of the letters
we have learned.

* Note that the majority of loanwords from English are transliterated into Korean with aspirated consonants (particularly ㅋ, ㅍ, ㅌ), as in the next examples:

Examples

컴퓨터 computer		프린터 printer
휴대폰 cell phone		토마토 tomato
햄버거 hamburger		피아노 piano
토스트 toast		초콜릿 chocolate
모니터 monitor		태블릿 tablet

* Before finishing this section dedicated to the Korean alphabet, let's go over some of the most common mistakes made when writing Korean.

letters written properly:

ㅁ   ㄹ   ㄴ

letters written in the wrong way:

ㅁ⊕   ㄹ⊕   ㄴ⊕

Some features of the Korean language

1 **Verbs** The verb **always comes at the end** of the sentence. All verbs end in -다, so if we take out this syllable, we generally obtain the stem/root. For example, the stem of the verb to go (가다) is 가-, while that of the verb to read (읽다) is 읽-.

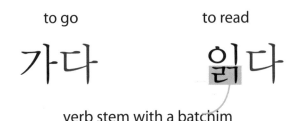

to go   to read

가다   읽다

verb stem with a batchim

| Exercise 7 | In the verbs below, identify the verb stem and state whether it has a batchim. (e.g., 만들다, the verb stem is 만들, and it has a batchim (ㄹ)) |

1) 가다   **2)** 밝다   **3)** 뵙다   **4)** 듣다   **5)** 크다

6) 먹다   **7)** 읽다   **8)** 옮다   **9)** 타다   **10)** 돌다

In Korean there are several categories of verbs:

1. action verbs: to eat, to read, to study; 먹다, 읽다, 공부하다
2. motion verbs: to go, to come, to attend; 가다, 오다, 참석하다
3. status verbs : to exist/not exist; 있다, 없다
4. the "to be" and "not to be" verbs: 이다, 아니다
5. adjectival verbs, also called descriptive verbs: be beautiful, to be busy; 예쁘다, 바쁘다

2 Linguistic protocol All verbs must be conjugated using the appropriate level of speech - that is reflecting the context. There are three main levels of speech (or level of formality):

1. formal (or in - ㅂ니다/-습니다)
2. semiformal (or in 아/어/여요)
3. informal (or 반말)

The level of speech depends on the context:

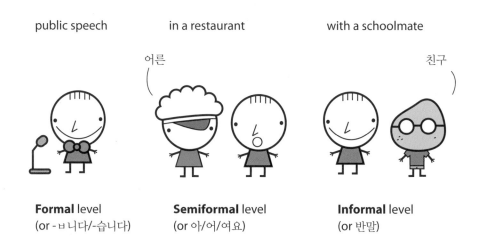

public speech	in a restaurant	with a schoolmate
	어른	친구

Formal level
(or - ㅂ니다/-습니다)

Semiformal level
(or 아/어/여요)

Informal level
(or 반말)

In addition, there is also a **"written form"**, which corresponds to a neutral level of formality. It is used when we are writing something that could be read by different people in completely different contexts. Another very important element to consider when speaking Korean is who the subject of our sentence is. If that it is a person superior in status (because that person is older or has a higher social position) or a person with whom we aren't acquainted, we must use courtesy forms (we will refer to these here as "honorifics") to show respect.

The level of speech depends on the context:

inferiority, respect   equality, confidence

We use the honorific form if the subject of the sentence is a stranger, is older, or is superior in status (e.g., King Sejong, an elder brother, an aunt, an aged person)

We use the flat form (without honorifics) if the subject of the sentence is a friend, a person of the same age, a younger person, or someone with whom we are acquainted.

* Some generations ago, honorific forms were also used inside families, and were used to refer to one's own parents, but nowadays it is more common to not use honorific forms in a domestic context.

③ Particles Certain parts of speech (nouns, adverbs, and verbs) can be followed by enclitic particles or postpositions, (often omitted in conversation), which indicate the function of the elements they are associated with (e.g., subject, object, topic).

Examples

e.g., I generally read the newspaper at six.
저는 (topic particle) 보통 여섯 시에 (time particle) 신문을 (object particle) 읽어요.

④ Punctuation marks The usage of punctuation marks in the Korean language is appreciably different from English. Let's learn here the Korean name for different punctuation marks and analyze how to use some of them.

Among punctuation marks used in the Korean language, but not in English, is the "middle point." It is used in the following three circumstances:

Punctuation marks
문장부호

Period: 마침표(.)
Comma: 쉼표(,)
Question mark: 물음표(?)
Exclamation mark: 느낌표(!)
Colon : 쌍점(:)
Quotation marks: 따옴표 (',"")

1) to link together two nouns in a list already separated by commas (수영• 수진, 영수• 순이)
2) to link together two similar nouns (충북• 충남)
3) in dates of historical relevance (3• 1 운동, 8• 15 광복)

There are several kinds of brackets: **1)** round brackets 괄호((),[]), **2)** corner brackets 낫표(「」) **3)** double corner brackets 겹낫표 (『』). Generally these double corner brackets are used when we mention the title of a book, single corner brackets are used for chapters within a book. See the following example.

Examples

『Flowers』에서 나오는 「Stars」의 "Broken petals"란 시행(詩行)을 가장 좋아한다.
My favourite verse is "Broken petals" in the poem 「Stars」 in the collection 『Flowers』.

⑤ Lexicon One of the biggest challenges for students of the Korean language is **the acquisition of the vast lexicon** (about five hundred thousand words), as well as understanding the usage and nuances of each word. For example, simply for the word "to be spicy," dictionaries list many possible variants:

맵다: to be spicy   매큼하다: to be just a little bit spicy

맵디맵다: to be very spice   매콤하다: to be slightly spicy

Korean nouns don't have gender, so to specify the gender of a noun we add the word "male" (남자) or "female" (여자), or the single (Chinese) words "man" (nam, 남) or "woman" (yeo, 여). The Chinese words are used as prefixes.

Examples

    e.g., haksaeng (student) ➡ nam-haksaeng (male student)
                                    yeo-haksaeng (female student)

Similarly, to specify the gender of an animal, you can use the prefixes 수 (su, male animal) or 암 (am, female animal). Korean nouns aren't always pluralized as they would be in English, but to specify that something is plural you can add the suffix 들 (deul).

Examples

    e.g., haksaeng (student) ➡ haksaeng-deul (students)

When talking about Korean vocabulary, we can't forget that up to 70 percent of Korean words can be written in Chinese characters (which generally means that they are derived from Chinese words). This means that the study of Chinese characters is extremely important for someone who wants to be proficient in Korean. From Chinese characters are also derived a number of **idiomatic expressions** composed of four characters each (which come from ancient tales or events). Let's see some examples:

Examples

천생연분 ➡ predestined relation
일석이조 ➡ killing two birds with one stone
팔방미인 ➡ one who is affable to everybody

Another significant particularity of the Korean lexicon is its richness in onomatopoeia, which forms an integral part of the vocabulary of the language. There are two different kinds of **onomatopoeia**: words that imitate sounds (의성어), and words that describe a movement or a shape (의태어).

1) 의성어:

부엉부엉: the cry of an owl
쾅: an explosion
콜록콜록: cough

철썩: splashing (of a wave)
쨍그랑: clashing

2) 의태어:

엉금엉금: to crawl
동글동글: rolling
뾰족뾰족: to be pointy
흔들흔들: swingingly
출렁출렁: to ripple

비틀비틀: staggering
꾸불꾸불: winding
비실비실: totteringly
긁적긁적: scratching and itching
딜렁딜렁: jingling

Unit 2: Exercises

Write the following words in Korean.

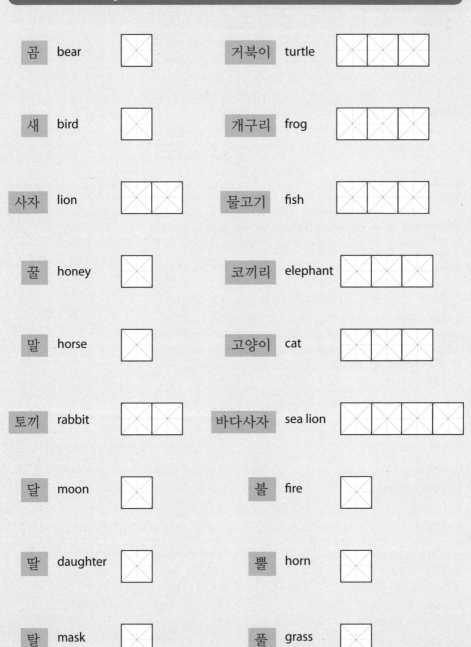

곰 bear

새 bird

사자 lion

꿀 honey

말 horse

토끼 rabbit

달 moon

딸 daughter

탈 mask

거북이 turtle

개구리 frog

물고기 fish

코끼리 elephant

고양이 cat

바다사자 sea lion

불 fire

뿔 horn

풀 grass

Unit 3

한글 3
Korean alphabet 3

- Diphthongs
- Phonetic rules
- Intonation
- Korean fonts

3

와 [wa]	공 zero	방언 dialect
워 [wo]	공 ball	부산 Busan
왜 [wae]	꽃 flower	사투리 dialect
웨 [we]	꽃가게 flower shop	서울 Seoul
외 [oe]	눈 snow	의사 doctor
위 [wi]	눈 eye	의자 chair
의 [ui]	대구 Daegu	쥐 rat
계란 egg	말 word	표준어 standard Korean
고추 chili pepper	밤 night	

Diphthongs

In this unit we analyze vowel combinations known as diphthongs.

오 + 아 → 와 [wa]   우 + 에 → 웨 [we]

When this diphthong is pronounced quickly the ㅏ sound is prevalent.
전화 →전아, 봐 → 바

우 + 어 → 워 [wo]   오 + 이 → 외 [oe]

오 + 애 → 왜 [wae]   우 + 이 → 위 [wi]

Exercise 1   Read the following words.

1) 괴물   2) 돼지   3) 과일   4) 궤   5) 퀴즈

6) 쾌감   7) 외국   8) 웨딩   9) 바위   10) 파워

으 + 이 → 의 [ui]

Some more tips on the pronunciation of 의:

❶ At the beginning of a word it is pronounced "으이"
(e.g., chair 의자 [으이자], doctor 의사 [으이사]).

❷ If it is found after a consonant, it is pronounced "이"
(e.g., hope 희망 [히망], pattern 무늬 [무니]).

❸ If there is no consonant before it, but it is also not in the first syllable, it can be pronounced either as 으이 or 이
(e.g., attention 주의 [주으이/주이]).

❹ It is pronounced as 에 when it functions as a possessive particle after a noun
(e.g., my house 나의 집 [나에 집]).

| Exercise 2 | Read the following words. | | | | ³⁵ |

1) 의식   2) 의식주의   3) 의논   4) 논의   5) 강의   6) 이의

7) 의상   8) 민주주의   9) 주의   10) 수의   11) 희망   12) 띄어쓰기

Phonetic rules

Now let's analyze some important phonetic rules of the Korean language. First, we need to remember that these rules concern only the pronunciation of the words, and don't necessarily reflect orthography.

In the case of a double batchim, only the second letter moves to the following syllable.

읽어요 [일거요]

❶ Liaison When a syllable ends with a batchim (other than ㅇ) and it is followed by syllable that starts with a vowel, that batchim will be pronounced as if it were part of the following syllable. For example, in the case of 밥을, the first syllable 밥 ends with a ㅂ (batchim), and it is followed by the syllable 을. So the ㅂ moves to the following syllable, and the word is pronounced [바블].

밥을   ⌢   바블

See some examples here.

Examples

³⁶

집이 ➡ [지비]

한국을 ➡ [한구글]

수업에 ➡ [수어베]

만들어요 ➡ [만드러요]

음악을 ➡ [으마글]

옷이 ➡ [오시]

29

Exercise 3   Write the following words as they are pronounced.

1) 가슴을	2) 돌아	3) 마음이	4) 서울에	5) 할아버님이
_____	_____	_____	_____	_____

6) 쌀이	7) 흙을	8) 밟을	9) 눈이	10) 인어공주
_____	_____	_____	_____	_____

2 Aspiration ㅎ When ㅎ comes before or after the consonants ㄱ, ㄷ, ㅂ, ㅈ, these consonants are aspirated, as shown below.

ㄱ + ㅎ → ㅋ   막히다 → [마키다]

ㅎ + ㄷ → ㅌ   좋다 → [조타]

ㅂ + ㅎ → ㅍ   법학 → [버팍]

ㅎ + ㅈ → ㅊ   좋죠 → [조쵸]

Exercise 4   Write the following words as they are pronounced.

1) 각하	2) 빻다	3) 놓지	4) 박해	5) 넣죠
_____	_____	_____	_____	_____

6) 낳다	7) 법하다	8) 굽히다	9) 좋대요	10) 국학
_____	_____	_____	_____	_____

③ Particularities of ㄷ **and** ㅌ When ㄷ and ㅌ are in the batchim position and are followed by syllables that start with 이 or with iotized vowels, they are respectively pronounced as ㅈ and ㅊ. This rule does not apply to compound words.

굳이 → [구지]　　　해돋이 → [해도지]

같이 → [가치]　　　밭이 → [바치]

밑이 → [미치]　　　갇히다 → [가치다]

In the last example, the ㄷ is aspirated (because of the ㅎ) and so becomes ㅌ. The word should be pronounced 같이다, but as the ㅌ is followed by 이, it is pronounced ["ㅊ", 가치다].

④ Voicing The consonants ㄱ, ㄷ, ㅂ, ㅈ are voiced when they come between two vocalic sounds.

ㄱ sounds like the "c" in "case" when it comes at the beginning of a word, but like the "g" in "game" when inside a word.
Examples: 가사 [kasa], 아가 [aga]

ㄷ sounds like the "t" in "table" when it comes at the beginning of a word, but like the "d" in "duck" when inside a word.
Examples: 더워 [teowo], 어디 [eodi]

ㅂ sounds like the "p" in "person" when at the beginning of a word and as "b" (like in "bubble") when inside a word.
Examples: 바지 [baji], 여보 [yeobo]

ㅈ sounds like the "ch" in "chat" when at the beginning of a word, but like the "j" in "joke" when inside a word.
Examples: 자요 [chayo], 아직 [ajik]

When we apply the voicing rule, we must be careful with the following two exceptions:

❶ some Chinese words don't follow this rule.
여권 [여꿘], 용돈[용똔], 발달 [발딸]

❷ When a verb stem ends in ㄴ or ㅁ and is followed by ㄱ, ㄷ or ㅈ, these three consonants are read as tensed and not as voiced.

신다 [신따], 신고 [신꼬], 신지 [신찌], 검다 [검따], 검지 [검찌], 검고 [검꼬]

This rule is also applied when a ㄱ, ㄷ, ㅂ, or ㅈ comes between a vowel and a ㄴ, ㅁ, ㅇ, or ㄹ:

갈가 [galga]
임대 [imdae]
공부 [gongbu]
반지 [banji]

| Exercise 5 | Write the words as they are pronounced. |

1) 아기

2) 건배

3) 귀지

4) 준비

5) 설비

6) 고기

7) 한국어

8) 공갈

9) 아비

10) 어부

11) 방지

12) 강국

13) 아버지

14) 농부

15) 지옥이

16) 지구

17) 바보

18) 붉어

19) 감기

20) 문제

❺ **Reduction** Every consonant can be found in a batchim position, but it is pronounced regularly only when followed by a vowel. For many consonants, it if the syllable is not followed by anything or it is followed by another consonant, one pronounces the sound of the head of the group those consonants belong to.

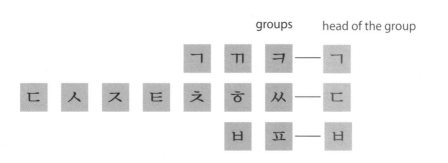

groups   head of the group

32

For example, the word 잎 (leaf), on its own, is pronounced "입"because ㅂ is the head of the group (because the head of the group is ㅂ). If 입 is followed by the word 사귀, it is pronounced "입싸귀." Only when 잎 is followed by a vowel is the sound ㅍ pronounced regularly.

Examples: 잎을 [이플], 잎이 [이피]

Examples

1. 꽃[꼳], 꽃이 [꼬치], 꽃을 [꼬츨]

2. 깎 [깍], 깎아요 [까까요]

3. 밖 [박], 밖에 [바께], 밖으로 [바끄로]

Exercise 6	Write the words as they are pronounced.

1) 갑   2) 잎   3) 옷   4) 빛   5) 부엌

_____   _____   _____   _____   _____

6) 국   7) 멋   8) 숲   9) 부엌에   10) 빛

_____   _____   _____   _____   _____

If not followed by vowels, the following words are all pronounced the same way.

빗
[빋]
comb

빚
[빋]
debt

빛
[빋]
light

* Only in rare cases a batchim follows this rule, even if it is followed by a vowel: 맛없어요 [madeopsseoyo], 못 와요 [mod-wayo].

33

6 **Assimilation** When the consonants ㄱ, ㄷ, and ㅂ
are in the batchim position and are followed by ㄴ, ㅁ, or
ㄹ, they are pronounced irregularly. Let's first analyze the
case in which the ㄱ batchim meets ㄴ, ㅁ, or ㄹ.

* This rule also applies to the consonants (ㄲ, ㅋ / ㄷ, ㅅ, ㅆ, ㅂ ㅈ,
   ㅌ, ㅊ, ㅍ, and ㅎ, which belong to the groups headed by ㄱ, ㄷ,
   and ㅂ (Please see rule 4, p. 32).

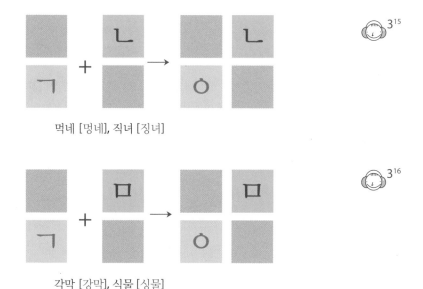

먹네 [멍네], 직녀 [징녀]

각막 [강막], 식물 [싱물]

In cases where that ㄱ meets a ㄹ, the ㄱ is pronounced
ㅇ, and the ㄹ will be pronounced ㄴ (For more details,
please see rule 2, p. 37).

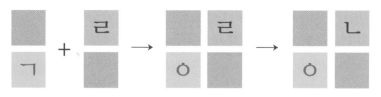

격리 [경니], 식량 [싱량 →싱냥]

We can apply the same rule to the group headed by ㄷ.

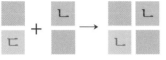   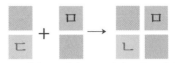

듣네 [든네], 뜯는 [뜯는]   꽃망울 [꼰망울], 못 만나요 [몬 만나요]

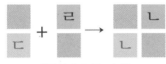

빗륙면체 [빈뉵면체]

Lastly, for the group headed by ㅂ, the ㄹ in the third example is pronounced [ㄴ] (For more details, please see rule 2, p. 37).

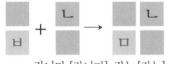   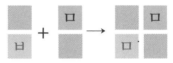

갑니다 [감니다], 갚는 [감는]   밥만 [밤만], 입말 [임말]

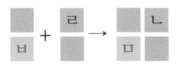

합리 [합리→함니], 법률 [법률 → 범뉼]

Exercise 7   Write the words as they are pronounced.

1) 칩니다   2) 갚네요   3) 밥만   4) 빛만   5) 국물

_____   _____   _____   _____   _____

6) 국립   7) 독립   8) 묻네요   9) 볶는다   10) 합리화

_____   _____   _____   _____   _____

11) 악몽   12) 좁네   13) 갚네   14) 디귿만   15) 덧만

_____   _____   _____   _____   _____

16) 씁니다   17) 봅니다   18) 맞네   19) 맛만   20) 먹는다

_____   _____   _____   _____   _____

7 Tensification When the consonants ㄱ, ㄷ, or ㅂ (or letters in their groups affected by the reduction rule 5, p. 32) are followed by ㄱ, ㄷ, ㅂ, ㅅ, or ㅈ, they are pronounced as "tense" consonants, or double consonants.

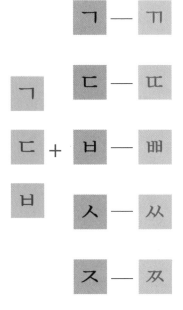

3²¹.

학교 [학꾜]
국밥 [국빱]
받다 [받따]
갚다 [갑따]
학생 [학쌩]
덥지만 [덥찌만]

Some Korean words always have a tensified pronunciation when in compounds. Examples include "가게" (store), "바닥" (floor/palm), and "등" (back).

palm of one's hand
손바닥 [손빠닥]

the floor of a room
방바닥 [방빠닥]

Other words take on a tensified pronunciation only in certain compounds. This is the case for rice (밥), meat (고기), and money (돈).

fish
물고기 [물꼬기]
pork (meat)
돼지고기 [돼지고기]

Exercise 8   Write the words as they are pronounced.   3²²

1) 먹지

2) 국자

3) 뜨겁군

4) 집도

5) 밥도

_____

6) 맥주

7) 각지다

8) 법적

9) 먹보

10) 볶다

_____

11) 악단

12) 학자

13) 걷자

14) 합법

15) 듣다

_____

8 Particularities of ㄹ Now let's consider some phonetic particularities of the letter ㄹ. When found at the beginning of a word, it is pronounced like the "r" in "rice." Two consecutive ㄹ are pronounced like a double "l."

* When transliterating into Korean a foreign word containing an "l," it is normal to use two consecutive ㄹ.

Examples

Cola ➡ 콜라, Italy ➡ 이탈리아

When pronouncing ㄹ, we must pay attention to **some particularities**.

1) When a ㄹ meets a ㄴ, the ㄴ must be pronounced as "ㄹ". 불나다 [불라다], 언론 [얼론]

2) When, in words of Chinese origin, the ㄹ is preceded by a consonant other than ㅎ or ㄱ, it is pronounced "ㄴ." 탐라 [탐나], 공란 [공난]

3) When, in words of Chinese origins, it is followed by ㄷ, ㅅ or ㅈ, these are tensified. 결제 [결쩨], 발전 [발쩐]

4) In some verb conjugations, when ㄹ falls in the batchim position in the stem, the first consonant in the verb suffix is tensified.

Examples

먹을 거예요 [머글 꺼예요], 먹을 줄 알아 [머글 쭐 알아]

| Exercise 9 | Write the words as they are pronounced. |

1) 신라

2) 심리

3) 감리

4) 발달

5) 전래

6) 결심

7) 법률

8) 침략

9) 결사

10) 벌낫

11) 길조

12) 망라

13) 결정

14) 갈등

15) 필사

37

9 Double batchim A syllable block can also hold two batchims. Both consonants are pronounced only when the block is followed by a vowel. Otherwise, only one of the two consonants will be pronounced. In some cases it is the first consonant that is pronounced; in other cases, it is the second.

> ⚠️ If the combinations ㄶ and ㅀ are followed by ㄱ, ㄷ, or ㅈ, they are aspirated
>
> 앓지만 [안치만]

Combinations in which the first consonant prevails.

³²⁵

ㅄ ➡ ㅂ	값 [갑] In some cases the ㅂ prevails, (e.g., 밟다 [밥따])	
ㄳ ➡ ㄱ	넋 [넉]	
ㄼ ➡ ㄹ	넓다 [널따]	
ㄽ ➡ ㄹ	외곬 [외골]	
ㄵ ➡ ㄴ	앉다 [안따]	
ㄾ ➡ ㄹ	핥다 [할따]	

Combinations in which the second consonant prevails.

³²⁶

ㄺ ➡ ㄱ	읽다 [익따] But if followed by ㄱ, the ㄹ prevails, (e.g., 읽기 [일끼]).	
ㄿ ➡ ㅂ	읊다 [읍따]	
ㄻ ➡ ㅁ	닮다 [담따]	

Exercise 10 Write the words as they are pronounced. ³²⁷

1) 값을   2) 몫   3) 넓지   4) 읊다   5) 흙덩어리

6) 붉다   7) 여덟시   8) 밟던   9) 많죠   10) 않습니다

10 Long vowels Some vowels used to be pronounced with a longer sound, in order to share a syllable from the rest of the word or to avoid homophony. This lengthening is still marked in Korean monolingual dictionaries by a colon, but a phonetic distinction is almost lost in modern spoken Korean.

밤 night	밤 chestnut		눈 eye	눈 snow
공 zero	공 ball		말 horse	말 word

38

⑪ Chinese characters As mentioned above, many Korean words written today with the Korean alphabet were **originally written with Chinese characters** (primarily words from China, and some developed in Korea and Japan). Some specific characters may affect the pronunciation of a syllable.

과(科) 기계과 [기계꽈]	내과 [내꽈]
권(券) 여권 [여꿘]	입장권 [입장꿘]
장(狀) 상장 [상짱]	초대장 [초대짱]
증(症) 후유증 [후유쯩]	다한증 [다한쯩]

Some other characters behave in an irregular way. In some cases they bring a tensification and in others they don't.

법(法) 사용법 [사용뻡]	방법 [방법]
증(證) 학생증 [학생쯩]	영수증 [영수증]
자(字) 한자 [한짜]	한 자 [한 자]
격(格) 성격 [성ː격]	자격 [자격]

Intonation

Besides learning the correct pronunciation of each word, it is important to pay attention to regional **accents** and **intonations** within sentences. In Korea, there are different accents, which differ from region to region. Try listening to the following track (3-31) and identifying the differences between a Seoul accent (the accent considered standard in Korea) and one from the southeast of the peninsula (spoken in the dialect of the Gyeongsang provinces, called 사투리 or 방언).

Seoul

Gyeongsang

1. First version: Seoul accent (standard Korean)
2. Second version: dialect of the Gyeongsang provinces

여보세요? 안녕하세요? 저는 안드레아인데요.

영희, 지금 집에 있어요?

아, 지금 집에 없어요?

그럼 이따가 다시 전화할게요.

안녕히 계세요.

The following tracks illustrate some common intonation patterns.
Listen to them and try to imitate the speaker's intonation.

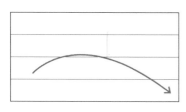

Affirmative sentences

1. 배가 아파요. I have a stomachache.
2. 친구가 와요. A friend comes.
3. 날씨가 괜찮아요. The weather is nice.
4. 어제 학교에 갔어요. Yesterday I went to school.

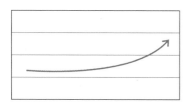

Interrogative sentences

1. 배가 아파요? Do you have a stomachache?
2. 친구가 옵니까? Does a friend come?
3. 날씨가 괜찮아요? Is the weather nice?
4. 어제 학교에 갔어요? Did you go to school yesterday?

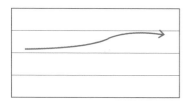

Imperative sentences

1. 밥 빨리 먹어! Eat quickly!
2. 얼른 자! Come on, sleep!
3. 가지 말아요! Don't go!
4. 오지 마세요! Don't come!

40

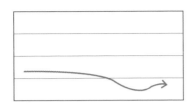

Exhortatory sentences

3³⁵

1. 같이 가요. Let's go together.
2. 어서 갑시다. Let's hurry up.
3. 내일 공부하자. Let's study tomorrow.
4. 가지 말자. Let's stay here.

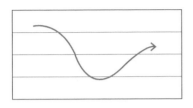

Exclamatory sentences

3³⁶

1. 너무 좋군! That's too beautiful!
2. 괜찮네요! Nice!
3. 그렇군요! Really!
4. 가셨구나! Damn, he left!

Note that in the following sentences, by changing the intonation the meaning itself of the sentence can change.

3³⁷

1. 어디 가요?
Where do you go?

3. 누구 만나?
Who do you meet?

2. 어디 가요?
Do you go somewhere?

4. 누구 만나?
Do you meet with someone?

When listening to Korean, we must pay attention to the speaker's tone, because it can alter the meaning. For some examples, let's listen to some sentences pronounced with a stubborn tone and some with a sarcastic one.

3³⁸

Stubborn Tone

1. 야~!
Come on!!!
2. 같이 가자~!
Come on, let's go together!!!

Sarcastic Tone

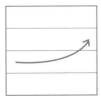

1. 좋네!
Amazing! (=very bad)

2. 아주 좋다!
I adore it! (= I abhor it)

41

Fonts

Before concluding this section on the Korean alphabet, let's look at a selection of commonly used Korean fonts. This can help to refine or personalize our handwriting.

바탕체 BatangChe	안녕하십니까? 한국어 노트입니다.
돋음체 DotumChe	안녕하십니까? 한국어 노트입니다.
굴림체 GulimChe	안녕하십니까? 한국어 노트입니다.
맑은고딕체 Malgun Gothic	안녕하십니까? 한국어 노트입니다.
궁서체 GungsuhChe	**안녕하십니까? 한국어 노트입니다.**

One of the most difficult aspects of writing Korean is to harmonize the proportions of syllable blocks. The more letters are in a block, the smaller each one needs to be written. Try writing the following words while focusing on maintaining the proportions within the syllable blocks.

삶은계란 Boiled Eggs

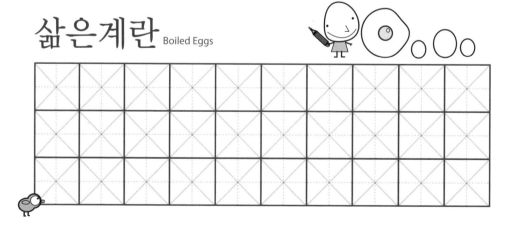

Let's memorize some basic greeting expressions, which also allow us to apply some of the phonetic rules we have learned.

안녕하세요?	Hi! (when we meet a person)
안녕히 가세요.	Bye! (referred to someone who takes his leave from us)
안녕히 계세요.	Bye! (when we take our leave from our interlocutor)
안녕히 주무세요.	Good night!
잘 먹겠습니다.	Good appetite! (before eating)
잘 먹었습니다.	Thank you! (when we stop eating)
다녀오겠습니다.	See you later! (while leaving home)
고맙습니다.	Thank you!
감사합니다.	Thank you! (more formal)
천만에요.	You're welcome!
미안합니다.	Sorry!
죄송합니다.	Sorry! (more formal)

Phonetic annotations:
- 잘 먹겠습니다: ㄱ+ㄱ→ㄲ, ㅆ+ㅅ→ㅆ, ㅂ+ㄴ→ㅁㄴ
- 잘 먹었습니다: ㅆ+ㅅ→ㅆ, ㅂ+ㄴ→ㅁㄴ
- 다녀오겠습니다: ㅆ+ㅅ→ㅆ, ㅂ+ㄴ→ㅁㄴ
- 고맙습니다: ㅂ+ㄴ→ㅁㄴ
- 감사합니다: ㅂ+ㄴ→ㅁㄴ

Exercise 1   Write the following words.

쥐   rat   ☒

말   horse   ☒

의자   chair   ☒☒

꽃가게   flower shop   ☒☒☒

의사   doctor   ☒☒

사투리   dialect   ☒☒☒

Exercise 2   Write the following words as they are pronounced.

1) 좋게

_____

2) 같이

_____

3) 막히게

_____

4) 국립

_____

5) 내과

_____

6) 읽다

_____

7) 법학

_____

8) 압박

_____

9) 빗살

_____

10) 신라

_____

11) 전래

_____

12) 침략

_____

13) 한자

_____

14) 학교

_____

15) 닮다

_____

16) 여권

_____

17) 성격

_____

18) 문법

_____

Unit 4

공부합니까?
Do you study?

The topic particle 은/는
The formal level of speech - ㅂ니다/습니다
The nominal predicate in an affirmative sentence

4

TEXT 1

먹습니까? 네, 먹습니다.
Do you eat? Yes, I eat.

공부합니까? 네, 공부합니다.
Do you study? Yes, I study.

춥습니까? 네, 춥습니다.
Is it cold? Yes, it is cold.

놉니까? 네, 놉니다.
Do you play? Yes, I do.

TEXT 2

저는 학생입니다.
I am a student.

저는 한국 사람입니다.
I am Korean.

책입니까? 네, 책입니다.
Is this a book? Yes, it is a book.

나무입니까? 네, 나무입니다.
Is it a tree? Yes, it is a tree.

The topic particle 은/는

The particle 은/는 follows to the topic of the sentence, which often corresponds to the subject of the sentence. We apply 는 to nouns without batchim, and 은 to nouns with batchim, as in the following examples.

Examples

Nouns without batchim

나 (I) ➡ 나는, 저는
벌레 (bug) ➡ 벌레는
엽서 (postcard) ➡ 엽서는

Nouns with batchim

사람 (person) ➡ 사람은
밥 (rice) ➡ 밥은
그림 (drawing) ➡ 그림은

Exercise 1 Apply the topic particle to the following nouns.

1) 값

2) 몫

3) 친구

4) 돈

5) 나무

_____   _____   _____   _____   _____

6) 돌

7) 쌀

8) 집

9) 사랑

10) 도서관

_____   _____   _____   _____   _____

The formal level of speech −ㅂ니다/습니다

In Korean there are three main levels of speech. Let's begin with the formal level, otherwise called the -ㅂ니다/습니다 level of speech (remember that the ㅂ before ㄴ is read [ㅁ], and so this suffix is read [-ㅁ니다/습니다]). Not all verbs behave in the same way, so conjugation at this level varies depending on the type of verb:

1. verbs with a stems without batchim (가다, 보다, etc.) add the suffix -ㅂ니다
2. verbs with a stems ending with a batchim (읽다, 덮다, etc.) add the suffix -습니다
3. verbs with stems that end in ㄹ (만들다, 물다, etc.) add the suffix -ㅂ니다

❶ Verbs with stems ending in vowel sounds (no batchim)

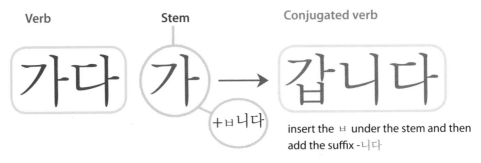

Verb   Stem   Conjugated verb

가다   가 → 갑니다

+ㅂ니다

insert the ㅂ under the stem and then add the suffix -니다

Exercise 2   Conjugate the following verbs using the formal level of speech.

1) 보다   2) 오다   3) 치다   4) 쓰다   5) 나쁘다

_____   _____   _____   _____   _____

6) 꾸다   7) 추다   8) 타다   9) 켜다   10) 예쁘다

_____   _____   _____   _____   _____

❷ Verbs with stems ending in batchim (other than ㄹ)

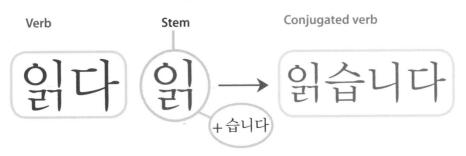

Verb   Stem   Conjugated verb

읽다   읽 → 읽습니다

+습니다

Exercise 3   Conjugate the following verbs using the formal level of speech.

1) 덮다   2) 밉다   3) 덥다   4) 춥다   5) 감다

_____   _____   _____   _____   _____

6) 괜찮다   7) 막다   8) 그렇다   9) 듣다   10) 맵다

_____   _____   _____   _____   _____

❸ Verbs with stems ending in ㄹ

Verb	Stem	Conjugated verb

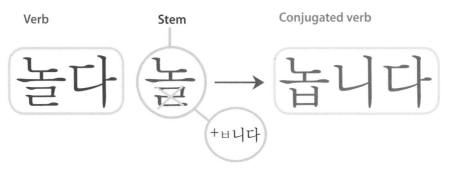

* ㄹ is always taken out when followed by ㄴ, ㅂ, or ㅅ. This rule is also applied to honorific forms, relative forms, to the causative form in -(으)니까, etc.

Exercise 4   Conjugate the following verbs using the formal level of speech.

1) 만들다   2) 불다   3) 들다   4) 멀다   5) 살다

_____   _____   _____   _____   _____

6) 굴다   7) 밀다   8) 널다   9) 끌다   10) 빌다

_____   _____   _____   _____   _____

The suffixes -ㅂ니다/습니다 are attached to the stems of verbs according to the typology of the verbs, and they allow us to conjugate a verb in the formal level of speech using **declarative sentences**. To make the sentence interrogative, replace the ending -다 with the interrogative ending -까.

	Declarative form	Interrogative form
가다	갑니다 I go.	갑니까? Do you go?
읽다	읽습니다 I read.	읽습니까? Do you read?
놀다	놉니다 I play.	놉니까? Do you play?

Exercise 5 Translate into Korean the following expressions using a formal level of speech.

1) Do you sleep? (자다)

_____

2) Do you turn? (돌다)

_____

3) Do you leave? (떠나다)

_____

4) Is it spicy? (맵다)

_____

5) Do you live? (살다)

_____

6) Do you open? (열다)

_____

The nominal predicate in a negative sentence

In an affirmative noun sentence, the subject is marked by the particle 은/는. The verb (copula) 'to be' (이다), conjugated in the proper level of formality, is placed at the end of the sentence. The predicative expression (a noun) is attached to the copula, as shown in the following scheme.

When a noun doesn't have a batchim, it is followed by a contracted form of the copula (-ㅂ니다, not 입니다), as in the following examples.

나무 → 나뭅니다
나무입니다
친구 → 친굽니다
친구입니다

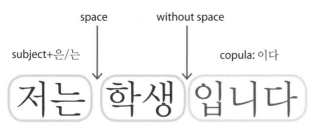

space   without space

subject+은/는   copula: 이다

저는 학생 입니다

predicative expression

| I | a student | am. |

Let's write

* In Korean, only nouns can be used in sentences like this.
 Adjectives behave like verbs in Korean.
 Correct: 저는 학생입니다. I am a student.
 Wrong: 저는 좋다입니다. I am good.

Examples

1) 친구 (friend) ➡ 친구입니다. (He) is a friend.
2) 나무 (tree) ➡ 나무입니다 (It) is a tree.
3) 괴물 (monster) ➡ 괴물입니다 (It) is a monster.
4) 펜 (pen) ➡ 펜입니다. (It) is a pen.
5) 바지 (trousers) ➡ 바지입니다. (It) is a pair of trousers.

We obtain the interrogative form by replacing "입니다"
with "입니까?".

Examples

⁴⁵

1) Is (he) a friend? Yes, (he) is a friend. ➡ 친구입니까? 네, 친구입니다.
2) Is (it) a pen? Yes, (it) is a pen. ➡ 펜입니까? 네, 펜입니다.
3) Is (it) a mouse? Yes, (it) is a mouse. ➡ 마우스입니까? 네, 마우스입니다.
4) Is (it) a pair of trousers? Yes, (it) is a pair of trousers. ➡ 바지입니까? 네, 바지입니다.
5) Is (it) a monster? Yes, (it) is a monster. ➡ 괴물입니까? 네, 괴물입니다.

Exercise 6   Translate into Korean using the formal level of speech.

1) Is it an egg?

2) Is it a chair?

3) Is it a book?

4) Is he a teacher?

5) Is it a horse?

6) Is it a tree?

Exercise 1   Conjugate using the formal level of speech.

1) 치다

2) 받다

3) 굴다

_____   _____   _____

4) 마시다

5) 낳다

6) 밀다

_____   _____   _____

7) 쓰다

8) 짓다

9) 빨다

_____   _____   _____

Exercise 2   Translate into Korean using the formal level of speech.

1) I am a friend.

2) I am a cat.

3) I am a cicada.

_____   _____   _____

4) Is (it) a lion?

5) Is (it) a frog?

6) Is (it) chocolate?

_____   _____   _____

7) Yes, (it) is a computer.

8) Yes, (it) is a baby.

9) Yes, (it) is a cucumber.

_____   _____   _____

Exercise 3   Listen and write.

4⁶

1)

2)

3)

_____   _____   _____

4)

5)

6)

_____   _____   _____

7)

8)

9)

_____   _____   _____

Unit 5

이것은 무엇입니까?
What is this?

Demonstrative adjectives and pronouns
The particle 의
Lexicon: names of countries
Personal pronouns
Interrogative pronouns

5

Vocabulary

가방 bag	볼펜 ballpoint pen	영어 English (language)	중국 China
공책 notebook	브라질 Brazil	이(이것) this	집 house
교수님 professor	사진기 camera	이어폰 earphones	책 book
그 that	선생님 teacher	이집트 Egypt	책상 desk
나라 country	선풍기 (electric) fan	이탈리아 Italy	충전기 charger
냉장고 refrigerator	스페인 Spain	인도 India	한국말 Korean (language)
드라이기 hairdryer	아버지 father	일본 Japan	한국어 Korean (language)
무엇 what	어머니 mother	저(저것) that	호주 Australia
미국 United States	영국 United Kindom	전기밥솥 rice cooker	

TEXT 1

5² 이것은 무엇입니까?
What is this?

이것은 볼펜입니다.
This is a ballpoint pen.

저것은 무엇입니까?
What is that?

저것은 공책입니다.
That is a notebook.

TEXT 2

5³ 이것은 누구의 가방입니까?
Whose bag is this?

이것은 어머니의 가방입니다.
This is my mother's bag.

저것은 누구의 책입니까?
Whose book is that?

저것은 제 책입니다.
That is my book.

Demonstrative adjectives & pronouns

In Korean, there are three main demonstrative adjectives: this 이, that 그 (something which is already known), and that 저. These adjectives are separated with a space from the noun they refer to. When they are used with the noun 것 (thing), they are written as one word (e.g., 이것) and take on the function of pronouns.

그

❶ may refer to a thing (or a person) that is closer to the listener than to the speaker (or that only the listener can see).

❷ may refer to a thing (or a person) already known both to the speaker and to the listener.

Demonstrative adjective		Demonstrative pronoun	
this	이	this	이것
that	그	that	그것
that	저	that	저것

Let's write

Examples

This person ➡ 이 사람   This cat ➡ 이 고양이   This book ➡ 이 책
That person ➡ 그 사람   That cat ➡ 그 고양이   That book ➡ 그 책
That person ➡ 저 사람   That cat ➡ 저 고양이   That book ➡ 저 책

This drawing explains better how to use these three demonstrative adjectives.

이   something which is close to the speaker and to the listener

그   something which is far from the speaker, but close to the listener

저   something which is far from the speaker and from the listener

> **Exercise 1** Translate into Korean the following expressions.

1) This horse

_____

2) This mouse

_____

3) That tree

_____

4) This chair

_____

5) That chestnut

_____

6) That cat

_____

The particle 의

Here we'll introduce the 의 particle, which marks the genitive case, primarily for indicating possession or belonging. As already explained (p. 28), in this case, the diphthong 의 is generally pronounced [에].

Examples

1) My mother's cat ➡ 어머니의 고양이 [어머니에 고양이]

2) My father's shoes ➡ 아버지의 신발 [아버지에 신발]

3) My elder sister's book ➡ 언니의 책 [언니에 책]

4) The doctor's ballpoint pen ➡ 의사의 볼펜 [의사에 볼펜]

> **Exercise 2** Translate into Korean the following expressions.

1) (My) friend's school

_____

2) The doctor's cell phone

_____

3) The student's mother

_____

4) The father's furniture

_____

5) The teacher's book

_____

6) The daughter's desk

_____

Lexicon: names of countries

If we add to a country name the noun 사람 (person, native Korean word, preceded by a space) or 인 a (Sino-Korean word, without spaces) we can indicate a person of that nationality.

미국 (USA) ➡ 미국 사람/미국인 (an American)
러시아 (Russia) ➡ 러시아 사람/러시아인 (a Russian)

한국 사람   중국 사람   일본 사람
한국인   중국인   일본인

When we want to use the names of countries as adjectives (e.g., a Japanese book), we can just put them before the noun without using the genitive particle 의.

a Japanese book ➡ 일본 책
a Italian clothes ➡ 이탈리아 옷

Finally, if we add the noun 말 (native Korean) or 어 (Sino-Korean) to a country name, we can indicate the language of that country.

Abbreviations

The names of some languages can be abbreviated. For example, for "English" we generally say 영어 (rather than 영국어, a word which is not actually used). For Japanese, one can use either 일본어 or the abbreviated version 일어, for French 프랑스어 or 불어, and for Russian 러시아어 or 노어.

한국 ➡ 한국어, 한국말 (the Korean language)
중국 ➡ 중국어, 중국말 (the Chinese language)

Personal pronouns

In this chapter we will introduce the personal pronouns: first individually, and then followed by the particle 은/는 or 의. When followed by 의, these pronouns become possessive adjectives (나=I, 나의=my). As you can see, these pronouns are **sometimes contracted**.

Pronoun	Meaning	Pronoun+은/는	Pronoun+의
나	I	나는 (난)	나의 (내) 🔦
저	I (humble)	저는 (전)	저의 (제) 🔦
너	you (informal)	너는 (넌)	(네 can also be pronounced [너] and [니]) 너의 (네) 🔦
자네	you (an older person talking to a person of the same age or younger)	자네는 (자넨)	자네의
당신	you (polite, often used between husband and wife)	당신은	당신의
그/그녀	he/she	그는/그녀는	그의/그녀의
우리	we/our	우리는 (우린)	우리의
저희	we/our (humble)	저희는 (저흰)	저희의
너희	you (plural, informal)	너희는 (너흰)	너희의
여러분	you (plural)	여러분은	여러분의
그들	they	그들은	그들의

* When we refer in Korean to something that belongs to us, in some cases one doesn't use the first person singular pronoun (나의 or 저의), but rather the first person plural pronoun (우리 preferably without 의).

my house ➡ 우리(의) 집
my mother ➡ 우리(의) 엄마
my country ➡ 우리나라
the language of my country ➡ 우리나라 말

In Korean, if you aren't well acquainted with your conversation partner, <u>it is impolite to directly address him or her as "you"</u> (너, 당신). It is better to use his name followed by an honorific suffix such as -씨 (Mr./Ms./Mrs.) or -님 (generally used in written conversations, including chat and email).

Mr. Andrea ➡ 안드레아씨, 안드레아님

Alternatively, there are a variety of titles/appellatives that can be used. (More are listed in the appendix.)

총각: young boy, bachelor (unmarried man)
아줌마: (softer: 아주머니): lady (middle-aged woman)
아저씨: mister (middle-aged man)
이모/고모: maternal/paternal aunt
학생: student
형/오빠: young boy, guy (literally elder brother)
누나/언니: young lady, girl (literally elder sister)

We can also address our conversation partner using professional titles, especially in working environments. Let's look at some of the most common: In this case, -님 is an enclitic honorific particle attached to the title.

선생 + 님 = 선생님 ➡ teacher
고객 + 님 = 고객님 ➡ client/costumer
교수 + 님 = 교수님 ➡ professor
작가 + 님 = 작가님 ➡ author
사장 + 님 = 사장님 ➡ president (of a company)

Interrogative pronouns

Let's consider two important interrogative pronouns:
what and who.

Pronoun	Meaning	Pronoun + 은/는	Pronoun + 의
무엇 (뭐)	What?	무엇은	무엇의
누구	Who?	누구는	누구의

Let's analyze some basic patterns with these pronouns.

1) What is this?

이것은 무엇입니까?

2) Who is this person?

이 사람은 누구입니까?

3) Whose is this thing?

이것은 누구의 것입니까?

Examples

1) Who is this person? ➡ 이 사람은 누구입니까?
2) This person is … ➡ 이 사람은 …입니다.
3) Who is that person? ➡ 저 사람은 누구입니까?
4) That person is … ➡ 저 사람은 …입니다.
5) This is my mother. ➡ 이 분은 제 어머니입니다.
6) Is this Andrea's father? ➡ 이 분은 안드레아 씨의 아버지입니까?
7) Whose book is this? ➡ 이것은 누구의 책입니까?
8) This is my book. ➡ 이것은 제 책입니다.

Exercise 3 Translate into Korean the following expressions.

1) Whose mask is that? 2) Whose chair is that? 3) Who is this doctor?

_____ _____ _____

4) Who is this person? 5) That person is Andrea. 6) Whose cellphone is this?

_____ _____ _____

7) Whose ball is this? 8) Who is this student?

_____ _____

Let's consider some more examples in which we use the interrogative pronoun "what?".

This is the teacher's book. ➡ 이것은 선생님의 책입니다.

What is this? ➡ 이것은 무엇입니까?
• This is a house. ➡ 이것은 집입니다.
• This is (my) friend's notebook. ➡ 이것은 친구의 공책입니다.
• This is a bag. ➡ 이것은 가방입니다.

What is that? ➡ 저것은 무엇입니까?
• That is a computer. ➡ 그것은 컴퓨터입니다.

What is that? ➡ 저것은 무엇입니까?
• That is a desk. ➡ 그것은 책상입니다.

Exercise 4 Write questions and answers about the objects illustrated below.

1) 드라이기   2) 충전기   3) 이어폰   4) 선풍기

이것은 무엇입니까?

이것은 드라이기입니다.

5) 휴대폰   6) 전기밥솥   7) 사진기(디카)   8) 냉장고

Exercise 1   Translate the following expressions into Korean.

1) My friend's cellphone

_____

2) My mother's refrigerator

_____

3) The baby's cat

_____

4) The teacher's notebook

_____

5) My sister's bag

_____

6) The flower's thorn

_____

Exercise 2   Answer the following questions.

1) 이것은 무엇입니까?

_____

2) 이 사람은 누구입니까?

_____

3) 이것은 무엇입니까?

_____

4) 그 사람은 누구입니까?

_____

5) 이것은 무엇입니까?

_____

6) 저 사람은 누구입니까?

_____

Exercise 3   Listen and write what you hear.

5⁶

1)

_____

2)

_____

3)

_____

저것은 자동차가 아닙니다.

That's not a car.

The subject particle 이/가
The nominal predicate in a negative sentence
Interrogative pronouns 무슨, 어느, 어떤

6

Vocabulary

가수 singer	무슨 what/what kind of	어떤 what/ what kind of	음악 music
공상과학 science fiction	방향 direction		자동차 car
공포 horror	배 ship	에로틱 erotic	자전거 bicycle
기분 feelings, mood	버스 bus	영화 movie	추리 detective (story)
기차 train	비행기 airplane	옷 clothes	코믹 comic
뜻 meaning	사랑 love	요일 day of the week	탱크 tank
마차 horse carriage	선인장 cactus	운동 sport	판타지 fantasy
만화 comic, cartoon	아니다 not to be	음료 drink, beverage	학교 school
모험 adventure	어느 which	음식 food	

TEXT 1

 이 의자가 좋습니까? 네, 좋습니다.

Is this chair good? Yes, it is good.

학생입니까? 아니요, 저는 학생이 아닙니다.

Are you a student? No, I am not a student.

저것은 자동차가 아닙니다. 자전거입니다.

That is not a car. It is a bicycle.

TEXT 2

저것은 선인장이 아닙니다.

That is not a cactus.

이것은 선생님의 가방이 아닙니다.

This is not the teacher's bag.

이 책은 무슨 책입니까? 음악책입니다.

What kind of book is that? That is a music book.

어느 것이 좋습니까? 이것이 좋습니다.

Which one is fine? This one is fine.

The subject particle 이/가

The particle "이/가" almost always marks the subject of a sentence. The usage of this particle is very similar to that of the particle "은/는", which we encountered in Unit 4, but there are **substantial differences** between the two. (**Check the appendix, p.151.**) For now, it is better to learn some basic constructions and to learn case by case where each particle is used. The particle "가" is applied to nouns without batchim, while the particle "이" is applied to nouns with one or more batchims.

* Korean personal names which end with a batchim can add an euphonic "이" before the subject particle. The name "은경", for example, can be found as "은경이" (name + 이) and also as 은경이가 (name + euphonic 이 + 가).
This rule can't be applied when a personal name is preceded by a surname. So, for example, "박은경" can only be found as "박은경이". This rule also can't be applied to foreign names.

Exceptions

❶ Some pronouns change if followed by this particle.

나 + 가 = 내가
저 + 가 = 제가
너 + 가 = 네가
(in spoken Korean, it is pronounced [니가])
누구 + 가 = 누가

❷ 이것이, 그것이 and 저것이 can be contracted to 이게, 그게, 저게.

❸ Besides the regular form 무엇이, the pronoun 무엇 can also be contracted to 뭐가.

Examples

Nouns without batchim

나무 (tree) ➡ 나무가
벌레 (bug) ➡ 벌레가
엽서 (postcard) ➡ 엽서가

Nouns with batchim

책상 (desk) ➡ 책상이
밥 (rice) ➡ 밥이
그림 (drawing) ➡ 그림이

Exercise 1 Add "이" or "가" to each of nouns below.

1) 값

2) 몫

3) 친구

4) 돈

5) 나무

_____

6) 마차

7) 기분

8) 집

9) 사랑

10) 학교

_____

The nominal predicate in a negative sentence

In Korean, some verbs have their own **negative form**. This is the case with the verb "to be" 이다, whose negative form is 아니다 (not to be). This verb is useful in making negative sentences with a nominal predicate — for example, "I am not ___" or "This is not ___." In this construction, we have to use both the topic particle "은/는" (which marks the subject of the sentence) and the subject particle 이/가 (which marks the nominal predicate). Let's look at the example below.

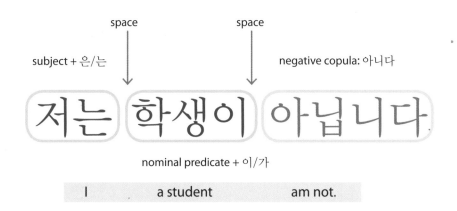

space · space

subject + 은/는 · negative copula: 아니다

저는 학생이 아닙니다

nominal predicate + 이/가

| I | a student | am not. |

Examples

I am not Italian. ➡ 저는 이탈리아 사람이 아닙니다.
I am not a singer. ➡ 저는 가수가 아닙니다.
He is not a professor. ➡ 그 사람은 교수가 아닙니다.
This building is not a school. ➡ 이 건물은 학교가 아닙니다.
This is not (my) mother's bag. ➡ 이것은 어머니의 가방이 아닙니다.
That is not (my) friend's comic. ➡ 저것은 친구의 만화책이 아닙니다.
That person is not a friend of mine. ➡ 그 사람은 제 친구가 아닙니다.

Exercise 2   Translate into Korean.

1) I am not Japanese.

_____

2)) Isn't this your friend's house?

_____

3) This is not a computer.

_____

4) This is not my dog.

_____

5) Isn't this person his friend?

_____

6) This is not a Korean book.

_____

Exercise 3   Write the questions and answers that go with the illustrations below.

1) 배

2) 기차

3) 자동차

4) 자전거

이것은 기차입니까 ?

아니요. 기차가 아닙니다.

배입니다.

5) 비행기

6) 마차

7) 버스

8) 탱크

Interrogative pronouns
무슨, 어느, 어떤

These three pronouns correspond roughly to the English "which" and "what," but there are some differences in how they are used.

❶ 어느: "which one" (among a finite group of things) or "to what extent"

어느 corresponds to "which one" and implies a choice among two or more (but limited) things.

- **Choice between two elements.**
Between the Chinese and Japanese languages, which one (어느 것) do you prefer?
To take the train, which way (어느 방향) do I have to go?

- **Choice among several elements.**
Which country …? ➡ 어느 나라 …?
Which period …? ➡ 어느 시대 …?
Which book (among several) …? ➡ 어느 책 …?

> **Memorize these three questions.**
>
> 어느 나라 말입니까?
> What language is it?
>
> 어느 나라 사람입니까? What country are you from?
>
> 어느 나라입니까?
> What country is it?

❷ 무슨: what, what kind of, what genre (type) (unlimited choices):

무슨 is used when we want to know about something and don't know the answer, and when our question doesn't have a finite number of possible answers (what a book is about, what happened, the meaning of something). We can use it with inanimate objects, but not with people.

*무슨 is also conventionally used to ask the day of the week.

> **Memorize these three questions.**
>
> 무슨 일입니까?
> What happens? (literally, what kind of occurrence is it?)
>
> 무슨 뜻입니까?
> What does it mean? (literally, what is the meaning?)
>
> 무슨 말입니까?
> What do you mean?

❸ 어떤: what, of what nature, with what kind of features?

어떤 is the adjectival form of the verb 어떠하다/어떻다 (how to be or what about it). It can be used in two different ways.

- **(as 어느) "which one"** (among a finite group of things):
Which food would you like? 어떤 음식을 좋아합니까?
Which beverage do you want? 어떤 음료를 마십니까?
Which garment fits me better? 어떤 옷이 더 어울립니까?

- **It can also refer to** features, contents, **the status, or the character** of a certain person or thing.
What kind of sensation do you feel? ➡ 어떤 기분입니까?
What kind of person is he? ➡ 그 사람은 어떤 사람입니까?

It is also used to refer to the typology or genre of a movie, novel, etc.

What kind of book is it? ➡ 어떤 책입니까?
What kind of movie is it? ➡ 어떤 영화입니까?
What kind of music is it? ➡ 어떤 음악입니까?
What kind of sport is it? ➡ 어떤 운동입니까?

As 무슨 and 어떤 are very similar, let's contextualize their use in a conversation.

A: What did you do yesterday?

B: I watched a movie.

A: What movie was it? (무슨 영화 봤어요?)

B: It was "The flower".

A: Ah, and what kind of movie was it? (그 영화는 어떤 영화예요?)

B: It is a horror movie.

What kind of movie do you prefer?

코미디 영화

액션 영화

추리 영화

로맨틱 드라마

공상 과학 영화

에로틱 영화

공포 영화

판타지 영화

Unit 6: Exercises

Exercise 1 — Fill in the blank with the correct particle.

1) 저__ 한국 사람입니다.

2) 제 친구___ 미국 사람___ 아닙니다.

3) 이것__ 제 가방__ 아닙니다.

4) 우리 의사___ 중국사람입니다.

5) 이 건물__ 우리 학교__ 아닙니다.

6) 제 친구___ 한국어 선생님입니다.

Exercise 2 — Translate into Korean.

1) I am not Korean.

_____

2) That is not her car.

_____

3) The teacher is not Chinese.

_____

4) That is not a comedy movie.

_____

5) This is not my bag.

_____

6) That is not my ballpoint pen.

_____

7) What do you mean?

_____

8) What kind of movie do you like?

_____

9) Among these two sweaters, which one do you like?

_____

10) Which country are you from?

_____

11) What kind of person is your friend?

_____

12) What day of the week is it today?

_____

Unit 7

책은 책상 위에 있습니다.
The book is on the desk.

The particle 에
The verbs 있다 and 없다
The prepositions of place
More information on the verbs 있다 and 없다
Lexicon: feelings

7

TEXT 1

⁷²   친구는 어디에 갑니까?
Where does (my) friend go?

친구는 집에 갑니다.
(My) friend goes home.

책은 어디에 있습니까?
Where is the book?

책은 책상 위에 있습니다.
The book is on the desk.

TEXT 2

⁷³   저는 시간이 없습니다.
I don't have time.

친구는 돈이 많습니다.
(My) friend has a lot of money.

저는 키가 큽니다.
I am tall.

저는 배가 고픕니다.
I am hungry.

The place particle 에

This particle takes the same form regardless of whether a noun ends in a batchim.

Examples

Nouns without batchim
병원 (hospital) ➡ 병원에
학교 (school) ➡ 학교에
교실 (classroom) ➡ 교실에

Nouns with batchim
세계 (world) ➡ 세계에
우체국 (post office) ➡ 우체국에
멕시코 (Mexico) ➡ 멕시코에

This particle performs the following functions.

1 It indicates that something or someone is **physically in a certain place**. It is generally used with state verbs, especially 있다 (to stay) and 없다 (to not stay), 존재하다 (to exist), and 살다 (to live), but also with other verbs like 놓다 (to lay, to put on), 넣다 (to put in/into), and 얹다 (put on, place).

I am home. ➡ 저는 집에 있습니다.
I am in Seoul ➡ 저는 서울에 있습니다.
Life exists on Mars. ➡ 화성에 생명이 존재합니다.
My friend lives in Busan. ➡ 내 친구는 부산에 삽니다.

Exercise 1 Translate into Korean.

1) at school	2) in China	3) in the city	4) in the United States
5) in Korea	6) in Spain	7) in Japan	8) in the dormitory
9) in the box	10) in Brazil	11) online	12) in that country
13) in the envelope	14) on the internet	15) in Italy	16) in this building

2 에 also indicates the **direction** in which one goes. We generally use it with the verbs 가다 (to go), 오다 (to come), 다니다 (to attend, to go frequently), 도착하다 (to arrive), and 이르다 (to reach).

I go home. ➡ 저는 집에 갑니다.
I attend the school. ➡ 저는 학교에 다닙니다.
Tomorrow I arrive in Tokyo. ➡ 저는 내일 도쿄에 도착합니다.
I reach the destination. ➡ 저는 목적지에 이릅니다.

* Be careful with usage of the verbs "to come" and "to go," as their usage does not always correspond to English. When we want to say that we are moving away from a place we always use 가 다. Therefore, where in English we say 'I'll come to your place', in Korean we say 'I'll go to your place'.

Exercise 2   Translate into Korean. I go...

시장
1) to the market

2) to China

도시
3) to the city

외국
4) abroad

_____

_____

_____

_____

5) to Korea

산
6) to the mountain

바다
7) to the sea

화성
8) to Mars

_____

_____

_____

_____

3 This particle also indicates **time (this will be further explained on p. 87)**, and it is used after the verb "to give" (주다 and similar verbs) when we give something to an inanimate object (for example, giving money to an institution or water to a plant).

The verbs 있다 and 없다

In this chapter we will introduce the verb 있다 (to be/to stay/to have) and its negative variant 없다 (not to be/not to stay/not to have). First, let's conjugate them using the formal level of speech.

있습니다 (I stay/I have)
있습니까? (do (you) stay?/do(you) have?))
없습니다 (I don't stay/I don't have)
없습니까? (Don't (you) stay?/don't (you) have?)

As mentioned above, the particle 에 is used with state verbs, including 있다 and 없다. Let's look at the following sentences in which it is used:

I am home (stay at home). ➡ 저는 집에 있습니다.
I am not home (don't stay at home). ➡ 저는 집에 없습니다.
My friend is at school ➡ 제 친구는 학교에 있습니다.
(My) friend is not at school ➡제 친구는 학교에 없습니다.

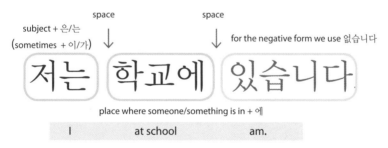

subject + 은/는
(sometimes + 이/가)

space

space

for the negative form we use 없습니다

저는 학교에 있습니다

place where someone/something is in + 에

| I | at school | am. |

Exercise 3   Translate into Korean.

1) I am at the market.

2) (My) friend is abroad (in a foreign country).

3) The student is in the dormitory.

4) My mother is home.

It is useful to introduce here the interrogative pronoun (어디 (where) and the adverbs of place 여기 (here, from the adjective 이), 거기 (there, in that place, from the adjective 그), and 저기 (there, in that place, from the adjective 저). These adverbs can also be used in Korean as nouns, and so become the subject (or other components) of the sentence. They can thus be followed by particles.

이 ➡ 여기   here/this place
그 ➡ 거기   there/that place
저 ➡ 저기   there/that place

여기 used as adverb ➡ 여기(에) 있습니다.
여기 used as noun ➡ 여기가 어디입니까?

Generally, when we ask where a person or a thing is, we can use either 있다 or 이다.

The prepositions of place

In this chapter we will introduce some common prepositions of place.

When we formulate a question to ask where something/someone is, we can use 1) 어디 followed by the particle 에 and then by the verb 있다 OR 2) place the verb 이다 after 어디 without spaces.

❶ 어디에 있습니까? 여기에 있습니다.
❷ 어디입니까? 여기입니다.

Be careful, because although the first construction can always be used, the second one can be considered inaccurate, or even incorrect in some cases. If we answer the question "Where is New York?" ("뉴욕이 어디에 있습니까?") using the verb 있다 (뉴욕이 미국에 있습니다), we have answered the question correctly. However, if we answer 뉴욕이 미국입니다, we have said, "'New York is the United States."

위
on

아래/밑
under

앞
in front of

뒤
behind

옆
beside

밖
outside of

왼쪽
on the left

오른쪽
on the right

안/속
inside

The following construct shows us how to use the prepositions of place inside a sentence.

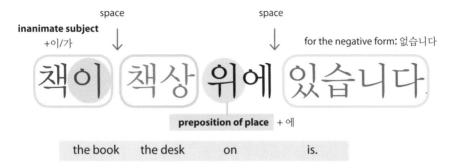

* The prepositions 안 and 속 are very similar.

속 generally refers to something that is **enclosed**, **enveloped**, or **contained** in something else.

Example: 옷장 속 (inside the wardrobe), 서랍 속 (inside the drawer), 봉투 속 inside the envelope

안 generally is used with **places or buildings** rather than with objects.

Example: 안 (inside the building), 방 안에 (inside the room), 집 안에 (inside the home)

In many cases, the two can be used interchangeably.

상자 **안**에/상자 **속**에 (in a box)

가방 **안**에/**속**에 (in a bag)

| Exercise 4 | Translate into Korean. |

1) The computer is on the chair.

_____

2) The trees are outside of the window.
창문
_____

3) My friend is in the room.

_____

4) The bag is inside the wardrobe.
가방   옷장
_____

5) The cat is to the right of the book.

_____

6) I am in front of the table.
식탁/테이블
_____

7) Japan is beside Korea.

_____

8) The charger is to the left of the pen.

_____

More information on the verbs 있다 and 없다

As mentioned earlier, the verbs 있다 and 없다, besides "to be" or "to stay," can also mean "to have." When used in this way, we must also use in the sentence both the topic and the subject particles. **The person who has/possesses** something is marked by the particle 은/는, and **the possessed** thing is marked by the particle 이/가, as illustrated in the next construct. Translating this sentence literally, it would sound like " 1. regarding a certain person(+ 은/는) 2. something (이/가) 3. is/stays/is possessed".

* Don't forget that in Korean there are also other verbs that specifically mean "to possess, to have, to hold," for example 가지다 or 소유하다.

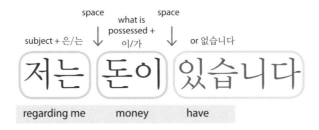

Let's apply this rule to some more examples.

I have a dog. ➡ 저는 강아지가 있습니다.
He doesn't have a house. ➡ 그 사람은 집이 없습니다.
(My) brother has a Korean friend. ➡ 동생은 한국 친구가 있습니다.
(My) Korean friend doesn't have a younger brother. ➡한국 친구는 동생이 없습니다.

| Exercise 5 | Translate into Korean. |

1) I have time.

2) I have a computer.

3) (My) friend has a book.

4) The teacher doesn't have a comic book.

5) I don't have money.
（돈）

6) Does the father have a cellphone?

An analogue construct can be used to **adjective verbs** in expressions to describe the features of a certain subject. For example, to say "I am tall," we use a formula which can be literally translated as: "Concerning me height/stature is tall."

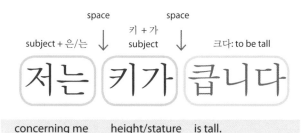

space	space	
subject + 은/는 ↓	키 + 가 subject ↓	크다: to be tall

저는   키가   큽니다

concerning me	height/stature	is tall.

Let's apply this rule to some more examples.

I am hungry. ➡ 저는 배가 고픕니다.
I am thirsty. ➡ 저는 목이 마릅니다.
I am short. ➡ 저는 키가 작습니다
I have long hair. ➡ 저는 머리카락이 깁니다.
I am clever. ➡저는 머리가 좋습니다.
I feel happy. ➡ 저는 기분이 좋습니다.

Lexicon: feelings

Let's look at some words for feelings.

행복하다
feel happy

기분이 좋다
feel good

기분이 나쁘다
feel bad

놀라다
be surprised

아프다
feel sick

슬프다
feel sad

졸리다
feel sleepy

부끄럽다
feel ashamed

화가 나다
feel angry

무섭다
feel scared

피곤하다
feel tired

당황하다
feel abashed

Exercise 1   Translate into Korean.

1) I go to Japan.

_____

2) (My) friend goes to school.

_____

3) Professor Kim goes to Italy.

_____

4) (My) brother goes home.

_____

5) (My) friend attends school.

_____

6) The singer goes to Seoul.

_____

Exercise 2   Translate into Korean.

1) The book is under the table.

_____

2) (My) friend is at home.

_____

3) The house is to the right of the market.

_____

4) The market is to the left of the building.

_____

5) The school is beside the market.

_____

6) The city is behind the mountain.

_____

Exercise 3   Use the following lines to write about yourself.

_____

_____

_____

_____

생일이 언제입니까?
When is your birthday?

| The particle 을/를
| Cardinal numbers
| The particles −부터/−까지

8

금요일 Friday
내년 next year
내일 tomorrow
년 year
마리 counter for animals
마시다 to drink
만나다 to meet
목요일 Thursday
물 water

불 fire, light
사과 apple
사다 to buy
생일 birthday
수요일 Wednesday
시작하다 to start
신문 newspaper
어제 yesterday
언제 when

오늘 today
오전 AM
오후 PM
올해 this year
원 won
월 month
월요일 Monday
일 day
일어나다 to get up

일요일 Sunday
작년 last year
잔 counter for cups
커피 coffee
켜다 to turn on
키우다 to raise/to breed (animals)
토요일 Saturday
화요일 Tuesday
휴가 holiday

TEXT 1

저는 사과를 한 개 삽니다.
I buy an apple.

저는 친구를 한 명 만납니다.
I meet a friend.

커피를 몇 잔 마십니까?
How many coffees do you drink?

그는 강아지를 몇 마리 키웁니까?
How many dogs does he have?

TEXT 2

몇 시부터 몇 시까지 공부합니까?
What time are you studying?

생일이 언제입니까?
When is your birthday?

제 생일은 10월 3일입니다.
My birthday is October 3.

오늘은 무슨 요일입니까?
What day of the week is today?

오늘은 금요일입니다.
Today is Friday.

The object particle 을/를

In this unit we'll introduce the particle 을/를, which indicates the **object** of a sentence. The particle 를 follows nouns without batchim and 을 follows those with a batchim, as in the following examples.

Examples

Nouns without batchim

나, 저 (I) ➡ 나를, 저를
벌레 (insect) ➡ 벌레를
엽서 (postcard) ➡ 엽서를

Nouns with batchim

사람 (person) ➡ 사람을
밥 (rice) ➡ 밥을
그림 (drawing) ➡ 그림을

Exercise 1   Use the correct object particle with the following nouns.

1) 값   2) 몫   3) 친구   4) 돈   5) 나무

_____   _____   _____   _____   _____

6) 돌   7) 쌀   8) 집   9) 사랑   10) 도서관

_____   _____   _____   _____   _____

---

* Some verbs that are transitive in English are intransitive in Korean, and vice versa. For example "to go on a trip" in Korean is "여행을 가다" In this sense, "가다" (to go) is used as a transitive verb.

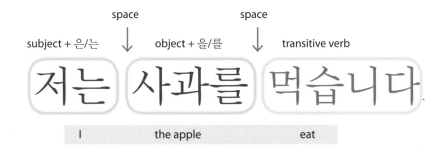

subject + 은/는   ↓ space   object + 을/를   ↓ space   transitive verb

저는 사과를 먹습니다

I   the apple   eat

I eat an apple a day. ➡ 저는 하루에 사과 하나를 먹습니다.

I drink water. ➡ 저는 물을 마십니다.

I read a newspaper. ➡저는 신문을 읽습니다.

I turn on the light. ➡ 저는 불을 켭니다.

Cardinal numbers

In Korean, there are two series of cardinal numbers: those that derive from Chinese (Sino-Korean numbers), and a set of native Korean numbers. The Korean numbers stop at 99, while the Sino-Korean numbers continue beyond 100.

Native Korean numbers

1 하나➡ 한	**11** 열 하나	**20** 스물
2 둘➡ 두	**12** 열 둘	**30** 서른
3 셋➡ 세	**13** 열 셋	**40** 마흔
4 넷➡네	**14** 열 넷	**50** 쉰
5 다섯	**15** 열 다섯	**60** 예순
6 여섯	**16** 열 여섯	**70** 일흔
7 일곱	**17** 열 일곱	**80** 여든
8 여덟	**18** 열 여덟	**90** 아흔
9 아홉	**19** 열 아홉	
10 열		

It is preferable to apply the particle not to the classifier but to the noun. Thus, 친구를 한 명 만납니다 is better than 친구 한 명을 만납니다 (to avoid the emphasizing the number rather than the friend). In written Korean it is also possible to use the classifier before the noun, and then add the particle 의 after the noun:

다섯 명의 친구를 만납니다.

These numbers are used mostly with **classifiers** (counters), which categorize the various objects into groups (like when we say in English "a pair of pants", "a cup of coffee," etc.). There are several classifiers that allow us to count things, people, and animals according to the categories they belong to.

* When a native Korean number is followed by a classifier, it is used in the contracted form (above, indicated by orange arrows: 한, 두. . .). Remember that it is preferable to leave a space after native Korean numbers, and to write them in letters and not in numerals.

Examples

To count people we use the classifier 명 (or sometimes the noun 사람): 한 명 (one person), 두 명 (two people), 세 명 (three people), 네 명 (four people), 다섯 명 (five people), etc.

> I have five friends. ➡ 저는 친구가 다섯 명 있습니다.
> In this classroom there are four students. ➡ 이 교실에 학생이 네 명 있습니다.

The classifier used count animals is 마리. So we can count animals as follows: 한 마리, 두 마리, 세 마리, 네 마리, 다섯 마리, 여섯 마리, etc.

> I have a dog. ➡ 저는 강아지를 한 마리 키웁니다.
> I see two penguins. ➡ 저는 펭귄을 두 마리 봅니다.

병
bottles

Here are the main classifiers in Korean:

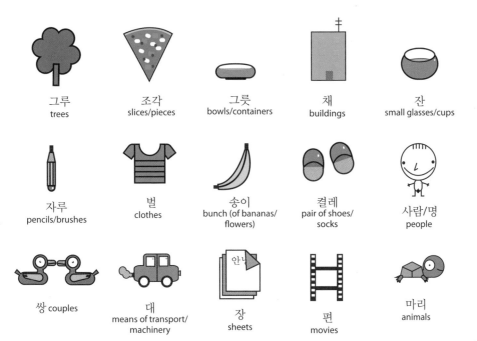

| 그루 trees | 조각 slices/pieces | 그릇 bowls/containers | 채 buildings | 잔 small glasses/cups |

| 자루 pencils/brushes | 벌 clothes | 송이 bunch (of bananas/ flowers) | 켤레 pair of shoes/ socks | 사람/명 people |

| 쌍 couples | 대 means of transport/ machinery | 장 sheets | 편 movies | 마리 animals |

To ask how many things there are, we can use the interrogative adjective 몇 (how many).

가족이 모두 몇 명입니까? How many people are (there in) your family?
커피를 보통 몇 잔 마십니까? How many cups of coffee do you usually drink?

Apart from the above classifiers, there is also a general one, 개, used for **objects that don't fall into any other category**.

e.g., chair: 의자 한 개, 의자 두 개

Another important classifier is 살 (year of life), used to count age. To ask someone's age in Korean we can say: 몇 살입니까? The answer can be: 한 살입니다 (I am one year old.), 두 살입니다 (I am two years old.), 열다섯 살입니다 (I am fifteen years old.), 스무 살입니다 (I am twenty years old.), etc.

| Exercise 2 | Translate into Korean. |

1) two dogs   2) three cups   3) five sheets   4) ten computers

_____   _____   _____   _____

5) twelve houses   6) fifteen chairs   7) two slices   8) six pairs of shoes

_____   _____   _____   _____

Hours, as well, have a specific classifier. When we refer to hours for telling time (e.g., Let's meet at 5 o'clock.), we use the classifier 시. When we refer to hours to express duration (e.g., We met for two hours.), then we use the classifier 시간.

* To specify am or pm, we can use the words 오전(am) or 오후 (pm) before the time. Koreans also might precede the times with words such as "evening" or "night."

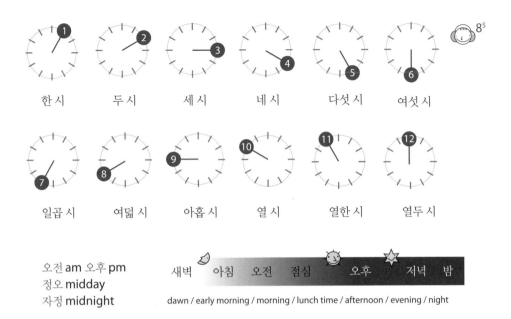

한 시   두 시   세 시   네 시   다섯 시   여섯 시

일곱 시   여덟 시   아홉 시   열 시   열한 시   열두 시

오전 am 오후 pm
정오 midday
자정 midnight

새벽   아침   오전   점심   오후   저녁   밤

dawn / early morning / morning / lunch time / afternoon / evening / night

For the earliest hours of the morning, we use the word 새벽 which literally means "dawn." Time expressions take the particle 에.

> I go to school at three o' clock. ➡ 3(세)시에 학교에 갑니다.
> I get up at eleven o' clock. ➡ 11(열 한)시에 일어납니다.

시간 indicates duration, and can be followed by 동안 (during). For example, we can say 한 시간동안 (for one hour). If we formulate a question referring to the duration of something, we use the interrogative adverb 얼마나 (how, how long).

> How long do you study? ➡ 공부를 얼마나 (얼마 동안)합니까?
> I study for one hour. ➡ 한시간 (동안) 공부합니다.

In addition to the native Korean numbers, the Sino-Korean numbers are also widely used.

Sino-Korean numbers

🐵8⁶

1 일	**11** 십일	**20** 이십
2 이	**12** 십이	**30** 삼십
3 삼	**13** 십삼	**40** 사십
4 사	**14** 십사	**50** 오십
5 오	**15** 십오	**60** 육십
6 육	**16** 십육 [심뉵]	**70** 칠십
7 칠	**17** 십칠	**80** 팔십
8 팔	**18** 십팔	**90** 구십
9 구	**19** 십구	
10 십		

* Only in this series does one find zero, which in Korean is called
공 or 영.

These Sino-Korean numbers are used to indicate minutes (분) and seconds (초). This means that when we want to tell time we use native <u>Korean numbers for the hour</u>, and <u>Sino-Korean ones for minutes and seconds</u>.

* To express the meaning "half past the hour", there are two op-
tions. For example, 1:30 pm can be 1) 한 시 삼십분 OR 2) 한 시 반

Let's consider some other times.

1:24 am 새벽 한시 이십사분   3:23 pm 오후 세시 이십삼분
11:30 am 오전 열한시 삼십분   5:53 pm 오후 다섯시 오십삼분
7:10 am 오전 일곱시 십분   8:03 pm 저녁 여덟시 삼분

Exercise 3   Write in Korean.

1) 12:30   2) 6:30   3) 9:30   4) 3:12   5) 7:20

_____   _____   _____   _____   _____

6) 5:10   7) 10:12 pm   8) 7:35   9) 1:12 am   10) 3:23 pm

_____   _____   _____   _____   _____

In addition, Sino-Korean numbers are used to read **telephone numbers, sums of money, mathematical operations**, etc. Let's look at the structure of a phone number.

ⓧ 진동   ✉ 문자메시지   * 별표 버튼   # 우물정자 버튼

의 [에]   의 [에]

공공팔이   공이 ↓ 삼사오 ↓ 오삼칠칠

(0082) 02-345-5377

국가번호   지역번호   국번호   가입자 개별 번호
country code   area code   exchange code   personal number

Exercise 4   Write in Korean.

1) 02-1588-0055   2) 02-5532-4412   3) 02-3455-2999

_____   _____   _____

4) 010-5222-4588   5) 010-333-4587   6) 010-875-2412

_____   _____   _____

To read sums of money, one needs to know higher numbers.

100 백   **100,000** 십만

1,000 천   **1,000,000** 백만

10,000 만

* If a number starts with 100, 1,000, or 10,000, it suffices to say 백, 천 and 만 (and not 일백, 일천, and 일만).

Examples

1) 123 (백이십삼)

2) 2,345 (이천삼백사십오)

3) 45,678 (사만오천 육백칠십팔)

4) 987,312 (구십팔만 칠천 삼백십이)

5) 1,239,596 (백이십삼만 구천오백구십육)

Exercise 5   Write in Korean.

1) 24   2) 468   3) 1,369

_____   _____   _____

4) 71,234   5) 468,411   6) 1,245,136

_____   _____   _____

The Sino-Korean numbers are also used for dates. Remember that in Korean the date is formulated in this order: first comes the year 년, then the month 월, and finally the day 일 (for example, 1994년 4월 24일)

Be careful with the pronunciation of 년. When it is preceded by ㄹ or ㄱ, its pronunciation can change, as in the following examples.

1년 [일련]   6년 [융년]
7년 [칠련]   8년 [팔련]

The words 년, 월, and 일 were originally Chinese words, but they all have also a pure Korean equivalents.

년=해
year

월=달
month

일=날
day

In Korean, the name of each month consists of a number followed by the word 월.

1월
[일월]
January

2월
[이월]
February

3월
[삼월]
March

4월
[사월]
April

5월
[오월]
May

6월
[유월]
June

7월
[칠월]
July

8월
[팔월]
August

9월
[구월]
September

10월
[시월]
October

11월
[십일월]
November

12월
[십이월]
December

Note two exceptions: June is called 유월 (not 육월), and October is called 시월 (and not 십월). There are no exceptions for the days of the months, which consist of a number (from 1 to 31) followed by the word 일.

1일 (일일), 2일 (이일), 3일 (삼일), 4일 (사일), 5일 (오일), 6일 (육일), etc.

작년
2015년

올해

내년
2017년

2016년
this year

12월 ← 1월 → 2월

지난 달
last month

이번 달
this month

다음 달
next month

8⁸

일요일 Sunday	월요일 Monday	화요일 Tuesday	수요일 Wednesday	목요일 Thursday	금요일 Friday	토요일 Saturday
		1	2	3	4	5

지난 주 last week

그끄저께 three days ago	그저께 the day before yesterday	어제 yesterday	오늘 today	내일 tomorrow	모레 the day after tomorrow	글피 two days after tomorrow
6	7	8	9	10	11	12

이번 주 this week

13	14	15	16	17	18	19

다음 주 next week

| 20 | 21 | 22 | 23 | 24 | 25 | 26 |
| 27 | 28 | 29 | 30 | 31 | | |

According to the calendar, today is :

2016 년 (이천십육년) 5월(오월) 9일(구일) 수요일

Exercise 6   Write in Korean.

1) April 15, 1999   2) June 12, 1422   3) October 29, 1894

_____   _____   _____

4) June 5, 2016   5) November 30, 2003   6) September 11, 2001

_____   _____   _____

In Korea, age is calculated in a different way than we do in the West. A person doesn't turn one after twelve months of life, but rather is one year old upon being born. Because everyone "ages" one year upon the New Year, someone born in December is already two years old when January comes. If you want to know the effective age of a person (만 나이)- not his Korean age - you can ask:

만으로 몇 살입니까? How many years have you turned?
몇 년생입니까? Which year were you born in?

The particles —부터/—까지

These particles indicate the beginning (-부터: from, beginning from...) and the end (-까지: till, until) of a period of time, as shown in the following examples:

From today to tomorrow ➡ 오늘부터 내일까지
From Monday to Friday ➡ 월요일부터 금요일까지
From 1:00 pm to 4:00 pm ➡ 오후 한시부터 오후 네시까지

Exercise 7   Translate into Korean.

1) From three to four o'clock   2) From the day before yesterday to tomorrow

_____   _____

3) From last year to this year   4) From Friday to Sunday

_____   _____

Unit 8: Exercises

Exercise 1 — Translate into Korean.

1) I read a comic book.

_____

3) I study Korean.

_____

5) I meet a friend.

_____

2) I eat a hamburger.

_____

4) I buy a computer.

_____

6) I turn on the lights.

_____

Exercise 2 — Write in Korean.

1) April 12, 1999

_____

3) May 16, 2014

_____

5) October 20, 2016

_____

2) 145

_____

4) 1,457

_____

6) 23,466

_____

Exercise 3 — Write in Korean.

1) 8:30 am

_____

3) 9:05 am

_____

5) 11:10 am

_____

2) 3:34 pm

_____

4) 7:12 pm

_____

6) 9:12 pm

_____

Unit 9

잘 지내요?
Are you well?

The particle 도
The semiformal level of speech 아/어/여요
The semiformal level of speech for verbs with stems ending in ㅂ
Lexicon: clothes

 9

TEXT 1

잘 지내요? 네, 잘 지내요.

Are you well? Yes, I am good.

무엇을 먹어요? 밥을 먹어요.

What do you eat? I eat rice.

그리고 물도 마셔요.

I also drink water.

신문을 매일 읽어요? 아니요, 가끔 읽어요.

Do you read the newspaper every day? No, I read (it) sometimes.

TEXT 2

반가워요. 제 이름은 김은정이에요.

Nice to meet you. My name is Kim Eunjeong.

방이 넓어요? 아니요, 조금 좁아요.

Is the room big? No, it is a little bit small.

오늘도 추워요? 아니요, 더워요.

Is it cold today? No, it is hot.

내일 로마에도 가요? 네, 내일 로마에도 가요.

Tomorrow are you going to Rome as well? Yes, I'm going to Rome too.

The particle 도

The particle 도 can be translated as "too, also, as well" in an affirmative sentence, and as "neither" in a negative sentence. If this particle is applied to a noun which has the function of topic (1), subject (2) or object (3), it replaces the other particle (은/는, 이/가, 을/를).

저는 사과를 먹습니다. ➡ 저는 사과도 먹습니다. (I eat an apple too.)
저는 연필이 있습니다. ➡ 저는 연필도 있습니다. (I also have a pencil.)

In other circumstances, 도 will not replace, but follow the other particle.

저는 학교에 갑니다. ➡ 저는 학교에도 갑니다. (I too go to school.)

Exercise 1	Use the particle 도 with the following nouns.

1) 친구를   2) 집을   3) 일본에

_____   _____   _____

4) 중국을   5) 선생님이   6) 나무가

_____   _____   _____

We can also apply 도 to expressions of time:
오늘도 (today too), 내일도 (tomorrow too), 작년에도 (also last year), etc.

* If we use 도 twice after two consecutive nouns, it can be translated as "both . . . and."
I eat both an apple and a pear. ➡   저는 사과도 배도 먹습니다.

Exercise 2	Translate into Korean.

1) I also watch TV.   2) I also go home.   3) I sleep too.

_____   _____   _____

4) My friend is Chinese as well.   5) Both my friend and I read books.

_____   _____

The semiformal level of speech
–아/–어/–여요

Now let's look at the semiformal level of speech. Many Korean verbs behave irregularly when conjugated in this level of speech. Verbs whose stems end in **solar vowels** (아, 오) take 아, and all other verbs (in which the stems end with lunar or neutral vowel) take 어. To complete the conjugation, we add "the polite ending 요".

☀ solar vowels

$$ ㅏ, ㅗ + 아 + 요 $$

🌙 lunar (and neutral) vowels

$$ ㅐ, ㅓ, ㅔ, ㅜ, ㅣ, ㅡ + 어 + 요 $$

Let's apply this rule to some verbs, and try first with some **regular verbs** with stems ending in batchim.

stem in ㅏ

$$ 밟다 → 밟 + 아 → 밟아요 $$

stem in ㅣ

$$ 읽다 → 읽 + 어 → 읽어요 $$

Let's look at some more examples:

덮다 + 어요 ➡ 덮어요	갚다 + 아요 ➡ 갚아요	빨다 + 아요 ➡ 빨아요
붉다 + 어요 ➡ 붉어요	돌다 + 아요 ➡ 돌아요	빌다 + 어요 ➡ 빌어요
굴다 + 어요 ➡ 굴어요	풀다 + 어요 ➡ 풀어요	늦다 + 어요 ➡ 늦어요

Depending on the intonation, this form can be used in declarative, interrogative, and imperative sentences.

94

DECLARATIVE	INTERROGATIVE	IMPERATIVE
밟아요./읽어요.	밟아요?/읽어요?	밟아요!/읽어요!

Exercise 3 Conjugate the following verbs using the semiformal level of speech.

1) 몰다   2) 물다   3) 놀다   4) 팔다   5) 긁다

6) 걸다   7) 멀다   8) 갈다   9) 밀다   10) 불다

This conjugation is more difficult for those verbs whose stems end in vowels or diphthongs, as the meeting of two vowels may lead to **contractions**.

stems in ㅏ

가다 → 가 + 아 → 가요

stems in ㅣ

마시다 → 마시 + 어 → 마셔요

Each vowel and diphthong behaves in a different way. The new vowel can simply follow the previous one (e.g., 괴 + 어 = 괴어). It can also happen that the first vowel prevails over the second and absorbs it (만나 + 아 = 만나). Sometimes the two vowels are contracted to form a new one, called a diphthong (보 + 아 = 봐).

First case: no variation
외: 괴다 ➡ 괴어요 / 의: 씌다 ➡ 씌어요

Second case: reduction

아: 만나다 ➡ 만나요 / 사다 ➡ 사요　　애: 재다 ➡ 재요 / 빼다 ➡ 빼요

어: 서다 ➡ 서요 / 켜다 ➡ 켜요　　에: 메다 ➡ 메요 / 떼다 ➡ 떼요

Third case: contraction

1) When 이 meets 어 they are contracted to 여.

이: 보이다 ➡ 보여요 / 쌓이다 ➡ 쌓여요

2) When 오 meets 아 they are contracted to 와.

오: 보다 ➡ 봐요　　오다 ➡ 와요

3) When 우 meets 어 they are contracted to 워.

우: 치우다 ➡ 치워요 / 태우다 ➡ 태워요

Especially difficult is the conjugation of verbs whose stem ends in 으. If these verbs have a monosyllabic stem (e.g.: 크(다), 쓰(다), etc.), their 으 is replaced with a 어. In the case that their stem is polysyllabic, we have to consider **the vowel of the second-to-last syllable**, and that vowel will determine the addition of either 아 or 어.

stem in ㅡ

크다̶ → 크 + 어 → 커요

second last syllable vowel: ㅏ → + 아

바쁘다̶ → 바쁘 + 아 → 바빠요

second last syllable vowel: ㅓ → + 어

슬프다̶ → 슬프 + 어 → 슬퍼요

Exercise 4   Conjugate the following verbs using the semiformal level of speech.

1) 쓰다   2) 예쁘다   3) 뜨다   4) 가쁘다   5) 치다

_____   _____   _____   _____   _____

6) 가리다   7) 빨다   8) 삐다   9) 끄다   10) 움켜쥐다

_____   _____   _____   _____   _____

11) 삼키다   12) 벌다   13) 뵈다   14) 찌다   15) 지다

_____   _____   _____   _____   _____

16) 이기다   17) 내다   18) 갈다   19) 쏘다   20) 보이다

_____   _____   _____   _____   _____

21) 띄다   22) 세다   23) 아프다   24) 피다   25) 나쁘다

_____   _____   _____   _____   _____

26) 꼬다   27) 좋다   28) 베다   29) 꿔다   30) 추다

_____   _____   _____   _____   _____

The verb to be (이다) and not to be (아니다) are complete exceptions: 이다 becomes 이에요 (if the preceding noun ends in a batchim) or 예요 (if the preceding noun doesn't have a batchim).

noun with batchim + 이에요   noun without batchim + 예요

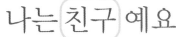

나는 선생 이에요   나는 친구 예요

* The verbs 되다 (to become) and 뵙다 (humble variant of the verb "to meet") also behave in an irregular way. They become, respectively, 돼요 and 봬요.

돼요! ➡ It is ok!
내일 봬요! ➡ Let's see tomorrow!

The semiformal level of speech for verbs with stems ending in ㅂ

Many verbs with stems ending in a batchim are irregular. Let's consider first those with stems ending in ㅂ (generally adjectival verbs). Only a very small number of these verbs are **regular**; among them is the verb 좁다 (to be narrow).

An **irregular** verb loses its ㅂ and gains 우, which is a lunar vowel and so requires the addition of an 어.

the ㅂ is taken out   we add ㅜ and then ㅓ

the ㅂ is taken out   we add ㅜ and then ㅓ

There is a small category of verbs that are "**doubly irregular.**" A verb in this category loses its ㅂ, but then gains an 오 and an 아. Among them are the verbs 돕다 (to help) and 곱다 (be pretty).

the ㅂ is taken out   we add ㅗ and then ㅏ

| Exercise 5 | Conjugate the following verbs using the semiformal level of speech. (The regular ones are indicated with asterisks.) |

1) 시끄럽다	2) 귀엽다	3) 맵다	4) 밉다	5) 매끄럽다
6) 덥다	7) 가깝다	8) 씹다	9) 곱다	10) 좁다*
11) 아쉽다	12) 춥다	13) 굽다	14) 곱다	15) 뽑다*

Lexicon: clothes

In Korean, "to wear" is 입다 (a regular verb that is easy to conjugate: 입습니다/입어요). The opposite verb ("to take off, undress") is 벗다. Besides these two verbs, there are also some more specific words, which are used according to the type of clothes being worn.

1) 입다 ➡ sweater, dress, overcoat
2) 신다 ➡ shoes, socks
3) 쓰다 ➡ hat, glasses
4) 끼다 ➡ gloves, ring

5) 차다 ➡ watch
6) 매다 ➡ necktie, belt
7) 메다 ➡ backpack, schoolbag
8) 두르다 ➡ scarf, shawl

Now let's memorize some of the most common types of clothes.

 내 옷  my clothes

티셔츠
T-shirt

스웨터
sweater

점퍼
jumper

장갑
gloves

팬티
underpants

반바지
shorts

바지
trousers

모자
hat

허리띠
belt

안경
glasses

목도리
scarf

양말
socks

넥타이
necktie

잠옷
pyjamas

치마
skirt

가발
wig

103

Exercise 1   Translate into Korean using the semiformal level of speech.

1) I read a comic book too.

_____

2) The singer also eats a hamburger.

_____

3) I study Korean too.

_____

4) My friend also buys a computer.

_____

5) I go home too.

_____

6) I turn on the lights too.

_____

Exercise 2   Conjugate the following verbs using the semiformal level of speech.

1) 아프다

_____

2) 모이다

_____

3) 굽다 ^{irregular}

_____

4) 채우다

_____

5) 익히다

_____

6) 맵다 ^{irregular}

_____

Exercise 3   Describe what the character is wearing.

_____

_____

_____

_____

Unit 10

음악을 들어요.
I listen to music.

The particles 에게 and 한테
The semiformal level of speech for verbs with stems
ending in ㄷ
The semiformal level of speech for verbs with stems
ending in 르
The particle 하고
Lexicon: family

10

Vocabulary

같이 together	마우스 mouse	서두르다 to hurry	좋아하다 to like
걷다 to walk	이메일 email	시험 exam	차 tea
계란 egg	묻다 to ask	싣다 to carry	치르다 to take (an exam)
고르다 to choose	믿다 to believe/trust	쏟다 to pour out	함께 together
다르다 to be different	받다 to receive	약국 pharmacy	화분 flowerpot
닫다 to close	보내다 to send	음악 music	흐르다 to flow
듣다 to listen/hear	보다 to see	이르다 to reach	
따르다 to follow	부르다 to call	자르다 to cut	
마르다 to be dry	빠르다 to be fast	조금/좀 a little bit	

TEXT 1

10² 선물을 누구에게 줘요?
Whom do you give the present to?

선물을 친구에게 줘요.
I give the present to (my) friend.

무엇을 들어요?
What do you listen to?

음악을 들어요. 그리고 영화도 봐요.
I listen to music and then I watch a movie too.

TEXT 2

10³ 배가 아파요. 의사 선생님을 불러요!
I have a stomachache. Call a doctor!

내일 시험을 치러요.
Tomorrow I take an exam.

학생들은 김 선생님을 잘 따라요.
The students pay close attention to what Mr. Kim says.

계란하고 토마토를 먹어요.
I eat eggs and tomatoes.

The particles 에게 and 한테

The particles 에게 and 한테 indicate an indirect object (to give something TO someone). 에게 is more common in written Korean, and 한테 in spoken Korean. They do not change based on batchim.

Examples

Nouns without batchim

나 (I) ➡ 나에게/나한테
벌레 (bug) ➡ 벌레에게/벌레한테

Nouns with batchim

사람 (person) ➡ 사람에게/사람한테
닭 (chicken) ➡ 닭에게/닭한테

The main verb used with these particles is 주다 (to give, 줍니다/줘요). It can also be found with other verbs such as 보내다 (to send) or 전화하다 (to call), etc.

I give a book to a friend. ➡ 나는 친구에게 책을 줘요.
I give food to the dog.➡ 나는 개에게 밥을 줘요.
I give a pencil to my sister. ➡ 나는 누나에게 연필을 줘요.
I send a message to my brother. ➡나는 동생에게 메시지를 보내요.

* Don't forget that if we give something to an inanimate object, we use the particle 에. (e.g., I give water to the plant /flowerpot).

Exercise 1   Translate into Korean.

1) I give a flowerpot to my sister.

2) I send an email to my Italian friend.

3) The friend gives me a pair of socks.

4) My brother gives a book to my sister.

The semiformal level of speech for verbs with stems ending in ㄷ

Among verbs whose stems end with a ㄷ, some behave regularly and some irregularly. Some of the **regular** ones include:

받다 (to receive) + 아요 ➡ 받아요   믿다 (to believe) + 어요 ➡ 믿어요
닫다 (to close) + 아요 ➡ 닫아요   쏟다 (to pour out) + 아요 ➡ 쏟아요

Some other verbs behave in an **irregular** way. This is the case with the verb 듣다 (to hear): it loses the ㄷ, and gains ㄹ in its place.

the ㄷ is taken out   we replace it with a ㄹ

걷다 (to walk) + 어요 ➡ 걸어요   싣다 (to carry) + 어요 ➡ 실어요

* Some verbs are especially tricky. They look similar, but based on meaning can have different conjugations, which may be regular or irregular.

  묻다 (to bury)
↓
묻어요

 묻다 (to be smeared with)
↓
묻어요

   묻다 (to ask)
↓
물어요

The semiformal level of speech for verb with stems ending in 르

In the previous unit we looked at the conjugation of verbs whose stems end in ㅡ. Verbs whose stem ends with 르, even if seeming similar to those with ㅡ, behave in a different way. With these verbs, too, we must distinguish between regular and irregular conjugations.

따르다 (to follow) + 아요 ➡따라요
치르다 (to take an exam) + 어요 ➡ 치러요

For the conjugation of these verbs, we must consider the vowel of the second-to-last syllable (just as we did for the polysyllabic verbs with ㅡ). If that vowel is solar, then we conjugate as in the following example of 빠르다 (to be fast):

Some verbs, like 이르다 (to reach) and 푸르다 (to be blue), behave in an especially irregular way. 이르다 becomes 이르러요, and conjugates differently than does the homonymous verb 이르다 (to be premature), which follows the conjugation pattern of other irregular verbs with 르 and becomes 일러요.

we add a ㄹ   we replace the ㅡ with a ㅏ

모르다 (to be unaware) + 아요 ➡ 몰라요   조르다 (to tighten) + 아요 ➡ 졸라요
마르다 (to be dry) + 아요 ➡ 말라요   자르다 (to cut) + 아요 ➡ 잘라요
고르다 (to choose) + 아요 ➡ 골라요   바르다 (to spread) + 아요 ➡ 발라요

On the other hand, when the second-to-last syllable has a **lunar or neutral vowel**, the conjugation will be as follows:

we add a ㄹ   we replace the ㅡ with a ㅓ

서두르다 (to hurry) + 어요 ➡ 서둘러요   구르다 (to roll) + 어요 ➡ 굴러요
흐르다 (to flow) + 어요 ➡ 흘러요   누르다 (to press) + 어요 ➡ 눌러요

The particle 하고

The particle 하고 denotes accompaniment (it is used to say, for example, "with" or "together with") or can be used to connect two or more nouns in a sentence. We apply it in the same form to nouns with or without batchim.

Examples

My friend and I ➡ 친구와 나
Coffee and tea ➡ 커피와 (홍)차
The computer and the mouse ➡ 컴퓨터하고 마우스
That man and that woman ➡ 남자하고 여자하고

* When this particle denotes accompaniment, it can be followed
by the adverbs 함께 or 같이, both of which mean "together." (e.g.,
"나하고 같이" and "나하고 함께" both mean "together with me").

Translate into Korean.

1) the cat and the dog   2) yesterday and today   3) front and back

_____   _____   _____

4) mother and father   5) I and the horse   6) the Korean and the Chinese

_____   _____   _____

If we use this particle to connect two or more nouns, we
must remember that these nouns can in turn potentially
have the function of the subject, object, etc, inside the
sentence. In such cases, the subject or object particle, etc,
must be applied only to the last element of the group.

space ↓   space ↓   the topic particle refers both to 나 and 친구.

나하고 친구는 학교에 가요

하고 connects the nouns 나 and 친구.

Let's see some more examples:

+ 을/를 ➡ 나는 배하고 사과를 먹습니다. (I eat a pear and an apple.)
+ 에게 ➡ 나는 동생하고 친구에게 선물을 줘요. (I give a present to my brother and to a friend.)
+ 에 ➡ 대학교는 뉴욕하고 시카고에 있어요. (There are universities in New York and Chicago.)
+ 도 ➡ 나하고 형도 떡을 좋아해요. (My brother and I like rice cakes.)

Translate into Korean.

1) I read a book and a newspaper.   2) I go to school and to the pharmacy.

_____   _____

3) He gives a present to me and to my friend.   4) Why don't you come with me?

_____   _____

* The particle 하고 can also be used consecutively, as in the following example: 책하고 연필하고 필통하고...

Let's look at two more important functions of the particle 하고:

1 하고 can be used with verbs like 같다 (to be like) or 다르다 (to be different), as in the following examples:

나하고 같아요. ➡ That's like me.　　나하고 좀 달라요. ➡ Someone is different from me.

2 If it is used along with the particle 사이, it can be translated as "between."

나하고 당신 사이에 . . . ➡ Between me and you . . .
그것은 책하고 신문 사이에 있어요. ➡ It is between the book and the newspaper.

Lexicon: family

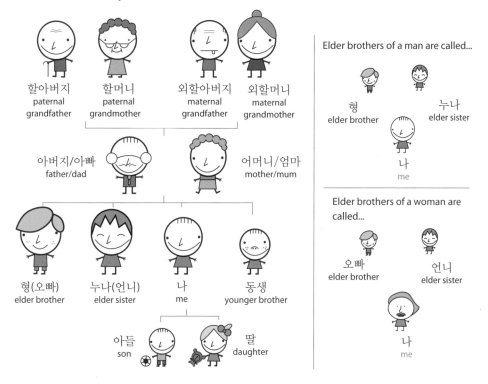

Exercise 1   Translate into Korean.

1) He gives the singer a book.

_____

2) I give an apple to (my) younger brother.

_____

3) I send an email to (my) friend.

_____

4) The doctor gives me a chair.

_____

5) My Chinese friend gives me a cellphone.

_____

6) My boyfriend gives me a flower.

_____

Exercise 2   Translate into Korean.

1) The computer and the mouse

_____

2) Yesterday and today

_____

3) The hat and the glasses

_____

4) Seoul and Busan

_____

5) New York and Chicago

_____

6) Italy and Brazil

_____

Exercise 3   Fill in the blanks with the correct particles.

1) 나__ 밥__ 좋아합니다.

2) 나__ 친구___ 선물___ 줘요.

3) 나__ 피자__ 사과__ 먹습니다.

4) 어머니__ 우리__ 돈__ 보내요.

5) 이 친구__ 일본 사람__ 아닙니다.

6) 나__ 책__ 읽어요.

Unit 11

공부를 열심히 해요!
I study hard!

The particle 에서
The semiformal level of speech for verbs with stems
ending in ㅎ and the verb 하다
Lexicon: the colors
Adverbs
Verbs ending in 하다

11

Vocabulary

걸리다 to take (time)	되게 extremely	신선하다 to be fresh	작가 author
괜찮다 to be okay	매우 really	아주 very	잘 well
그만 stop	보통 usually	아기, 애 baby	재미있다 to be funny
깨끗하다 to be clean	빨갛다 to be red	어떻다 to be how	죽다 to die
낳다 to give birth	살다 to live	얼굴 face	청소하다 to clean
너무 too much	숙제하다 to do homework	이따가 after a while	태어나다 to be born
다(전부) all	식당 restaurant	이야기하다 to talk	피곤하다 to be tired
도착하다 to arrive	식사하다 to eat	자다 to sleep	하얗다 to be white

TEXT 1

11² 친구가 어디에서 와요? 친구가 한국에서 와요.

Where does (your) friend come from? He comes from Korea.

책을 어디에서 읽어요? 책을 도서관에서 읽어요.

Where do you read books? I read them in the library.

기분이 어때요? 기분이 아주 좋아요.

How is your mood? My mood is very good.

하늘이 어때요? 하늘이 아주 파래요.

How is the sky? The sky is really blue.

TEXT 2

11³ 집이 어때요? 집이 정말 깨끗해요.

How is the house? The house is really tidy.

매일 공부를 해요? 네, 매일 공부를 열심히 해요.

Do you study every day? Yes, I study hard every day.

이따가 영화를 봐요? 아니요, 나중에 영화를 봐요.

Will you watch a movie soon? No, I watch it later.

보통 집에서 뭐해요? 보통 집에서 텔레비전을 봐요.

What do you usually do at home? I usually watch television at home.

The particle 에서

In this chapter we will introduce the particle 에서, which has two important functions.

1 **origin, starting location: from (a place)**

This particle is generally used with verbs such as 오다 (to come), 가다 (to go), 떠나다 (to leave), and 도착하다 (to arrive), as shown below:

I come from (my) house. ➡ 나는 집에서 와요.
The airplane comes from Korea. ➡ 비행기가 한국에서 와요.
(I) leave from Korea. ➡ 나는 한국에서 출발합니다.

* This particle can also be used with the particle -까지 (till, to), as in the following examples:

It takes four hours to go from New York to Chicago. ➡ 뉴욕에서 시카고까지 네 시간 걸립니다.

2 **It is used to indicate the place where we perform an action.**

It is used not to express that we are **statically in a place**, but rather that in that place we are performing an action, such as drinking, reading, etc. (Thus it can be translated as "in" or "at", as is the particle 에, but it is used with action verbs).

I eat at home. ➡ 나는 집에서 밥을 먹어요
I read books at school. ➡ 나는 학교에서 책을 읽어요.

* Verbs like "to sleep" (자다), "to be born" (태어나다), and "to die" (죽다), as well, imply action, so they also take the particle 에서.

When the subject of a sentence is an inanimate object, it may be marked by this particle.

삼성에서 이 휴대폰을 만들어요.
➡   Samsung produces this cell phone.

정부에서 관광을 장려합니다.
➡ The government fosters tourism.

Some verbs can take either particle, depending on the circumstance: if we use 에, we give emphasis to the stativity of the action, whereas with 에서 we highlight the dynamicity of the action.

저는 부산에 살아요. ➡ I live in Busan. (I am based in Busan.)
저는 부산에서 살아요.➡ I live in Busan. (I work and carry on activities there.)

* 어디 + 에서 is often contracted to 어디서.

Exercise 1   Translate into Korean.

1) He comes from Korea.

_____

2) The teacher comes from China.

_____

3) (My) friend and I eat lunch at the restaurant.

_____

4) My Japanese friend works in Seoul.

_____

5) I talk with the friend in the living room. 거실

_____

6) The writer lives in Korea. 작가

_____

The semiformal level of speech for verbs with stems ending in ㅎ and the verb 하다

Among the verbs with a stem ending with ㅎ, some behave regularly and others irregularly. Let's first look at the **regular** ones:

낳다 (to give birth) + 아요 ➡ 낳아요
쌓다 (to accumulate) + 어요 ➡ 쌓아요
빻다 (to pulverize) + 아요 ➡ 빻아요
좋다 (to be good) + 아요 ➡ 좋아요

Some other verbs are conjugated **irregularly**: we include

in this group the verb 하다 and words derived from it (for example 공부하다), which follow a similar conjugation. In the semi-formal level of speech we add a 여, which is generally contracted to 애:

하다 (to do) ➡ 해요
공부하다 (to study) ➡ 공부해요

Similarly, many other irregular verbs with ㅎ lose their badchim, and the final vowel is contracted to 애.

이렇다, 이러하다 (to be so) ➡ 이래요
그렇다, 그러하다 (to be in that way) ➡ 그래요
저렇다, 저러하다 (to be in that way) ➡ 저래요
어떻다, 어떠하다 (to be how) ➡ 어때요

To this group of irregular verbs we can add another small group of verbs used to indicate colours. Let's examine some of them:

빨갛다 (to be red) + 아요 ➡ 빨개요
까맣다 (to be black) + 아요 ➡ 까매요
하얗다 (to be white) + 아요 ➡ 하얘요
파랗다 (to be blue) + 아요 ➡ 파래요
노랗다(to be yellow) + 아요 ➡ 노래요

Lexicon: the colors

Let's examine here some nouns used in Korean to indicate colors. Generally, it is enough to put them before a noun (sometimes followed by the particle 의) to transform them into adjectives.

a pink pyjamas ➡ 분홍색 (의) 잠옷
a red hat ➡ 빨간색 (의) 모자

색깔
The colors

 하얀색 (흰색)
white

 주황색
orange

 회색
grey

 까만색(검은색)
black

 노란색
yellow

 은색
silver

 보라색
purple, violet

 연두색
light green

 밤색
brown

 자주색
violet

 초록색(녹색)
dark green

 갈색
light brown

 분홍색
pink

 파란색
blue

 살구색
apricot

 빨간색
red

연두색 (sky-blue 하늘색)
하늘색
sky-blue

Adverbs

The adverb is a part of speech that modifies or determines the meaning of the grammatical categories they refer to (mainly adjectival verbs). Not all adverbs are compatible with all verbs, and not all verbs behave in the same way when accompanied by an adverb. For example, 매우, 아주 (really) and 되게 (extremely) can only be used with adjectival verbs.

It is really good. ➡ 아주(/매우, 되게) 좋아요.
It is really pretty. ➡ 아주(/매우, 되게) 예뻐요.

Other adverbs can be used with all verbs: among these is
많이(many), which can be used both with adjectival verbs
and also with action and status verbs.

(It) is very good. ➡ 많이(아주, 정말) 좋아요.
(He) reads a lot. ➡ 많이 읽어요.
(I) have many. ➡ 많이 있어요.

Another useful adverb is 잘, which can mean, depending
on the context, "well," "often," or "a lot."

1) 한국어를 잘 해요. (I speak Korean well), 잘 자요! (Sleep well!), 잘 있어요! (Take care!)
2) 학교에 잘 가요. (He often goes to school.)

"Too much" is 너무 in Korean. It can be used alone or with
certain other adverbs (e.g., 잘, 많이) to strengthen their
meaning. It can't be used, however, with 아주, 매우, or
되게).

1) 너무 좋아요! (It is really good!), 너무 해! (That's too much!)
2) 너무 잘 해요! (You are really too good!), 너무 많이 먹어요. (I really eat too much.)

Two other useful adverbs are 그만 and 다.

1) If followed by a verb, 그만 means to stop doing something.
   그만 먹어요! (Stpp eating!), 그만 해요! (Stop doing that!/Stop it!)
2) 다 means "all" or "completely", but if followed by a verb, it means "to finish doing
   something."
   다 읽어요. (Finish reading it. Read it all.)

Let's take a look at some important **time adverbs** often
used in Korean. They generally come at the beginning of
a sentence. The meanings of 나중에, 이따, 다음에 , and 그

후에 seem very similar, but they are used in different ways.

이따 (가) ➡after a while (e.g., I will come to your place soon / in a couple of hours)
다음에 ➡next time (e.g., let's talk about that next time, in a situation where we meet regularly or on a schedule)
나중에 ➡later (e.g., let's talk about that later (next time we meet; if the timing is not specified, it can be soon or not)
그 (이) 후 ➡afterwards (e.g., after that the police came.)

Other important adverbs include... 자주, 자꾸, 보통, 일반적으로, 주로

자주 ➡often (I often go to the seaside.)
자꾸 ➡(too) often (Don't say that so frequently.)
보통, 일반적으로 ➡generally, usually (What do you usually do on weekends?)
주로 ➡mainly, mostly ("What, mainly, do you eat?")

Verbs ending in 하다

In Korean, there are two types of verbs that end in 하다: adjectival verbs (category A), and action verbs (category B).

1 category A) Adjectival verbs ending in 하다 (without objects)

These verbs can't be divided.

신선하다 (to be fresh)
피곤하다 (to be tired)
깨끗하다 (to be clean)
똑똑하다 (to be clever)

2 category B) object + 하다

These verbs are composed of a noun (almost always of Chinese origin), which is expressed as an action by the transitive verb 하다.

공부 (study) ➡ 공부를 하다 ➡공부하다 (study)
식사 (meal) ➡ 식사를 하다 ➡식사하다 (to have a meal)
이야기 (talk) ➡ 이야기를 하다 ➡이야기하다 (to talk)

If we want to use adverbs of quantity with these verbs, we must always be careful and determine which of the two categories the verb belongs to. If the verb belongs to category A, we just put the adverb before the entire verb.

However, if the verb belongs to category B, the adverb generally must be placed between the object (with or without 을/를) and the verb 하다, as demonstrated in the following scheme.

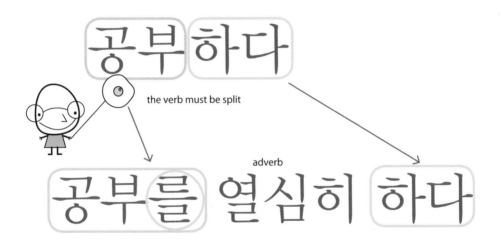

the verb must be split

adverb

숙제하다 (to do homework) ➡ 숙제를 다 하다 (to finish doing homework)
이야기하다 (to talk) ➡ 이야기를 잘 하다 (to talk well)
청소하다 (to clean) ➡청소를 그만 하다 (to finish cleaning)

Exercise 1   Translate into Korean.

1) I live in Seoul.

_____

3) I study Korean at home.

_____

5) I meet a friend in the library.

_____

2) I eat an apple in my room.

_____

4) I sleep at (my) friend's house.

_____

6) I read a comic book in the living room.

_____

Exercise 2   Translate into Korean.

1) I am very tired.

_____

3) I do lots of homework.

_____

5) I talk a lot.

_____

2) I am really sad.

_____

4) That book is really good.

_____

6) It is very cold.

_____

Exercise 3   Conjugate the following verbs using the semiformal level of speech.

1) 많다

_____

4) 빠르다

_____

7) 아프다

_____

2) 괜찮다

_____

5) 치르다

_____

8) 갚다

_____

3) 하얗다

_____

6) 예쁘다

_____

9) 옳다

_____

Unit 12

교수님은 무엇을 하십니까?
What does the professor do?

The semiformal level of speech for verbs with stems ending in ㅅ
The particle (으) 로
The honorific form, first part

12

TEXT 1

무엇을 해요? 손을 씻어요.

What are you doing? I am washing my hands.

집을 무엇으로 지어요?

What are you building the house with?

집을 나무로 지어요.

I am building it with timber.

교수님은 무엇을 하십니까?

What does the professor do?

교수님은 피자를 사십니다.

The professor buys a pizza.

TEXT 2

할아버지는 무엇을 하세요?

What is Grandfather doing?

할아버지는 신문을 읽으세요.

Grandfather is reading a newspaper.

지금 추우세요?

Are you cold?

무슨 음악을 들으세요?

What kind of music do you listen to?

The semiformal level of speech for verbs with stems ending in ㅅ

Among verbs with ㅅ, too, some behave regularly and some irregularly. Let's look at some verbs which behave **regularly**.

웃다 (to laugh) + 어요 ➡ 웃어요
비웃다 (to mock) + 어요 ➡ 비웃어요
벗다 (to take off clothes) + 어요 ➡ 벗어요

빗다 (to comb) + 어요 ➡ 빗어요
씻다 (to wash) + 어요 ➡ 씻어요
빼앗다 (to take away) + 어요 ➡ 빼앗아요

Verbs behaving **irregularly** lose the ㅅ in their batchim and gain a 아 or 어 depending on the circumstance. However, the vowels are not contracted, and do not combine to form a diphthong.

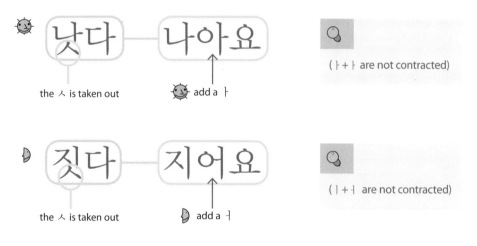

낫다 ─ 나아요

the ㅅ is taken out   add a ㅏ

(ㅏ + ㅏ are not contracted)

짓다 ─ 지어요

the ㅅ is taken out   add a ㅓ

(ㅣ + ㅓ are not contracted)

* The verb 낫다 (to be better) is the only ㅅ adjectival verb which behaves irregularly.

Exercise 1   Conjugate the following verbs in ㅅ using the semiformal level of speech.

1) 씻다   2) 굿다   3) 젓다   4) 잇다

_____   _____   _____   _____

The particle (으)로

The particle (으)로 is used with: nouns ending in a vowel (1) and nouns ending with ㄹ(2). All other nouns need an euphonic 으 before the 로 (3).

The particle (으)로 indicates the direction or the objective of a movement or a journey, while 에 indicates arrival at a determined destination. Therefore, when using verbs such as "to leave" (떠나다), "to go to study abroad" (유학가다), we usually use the particle (으)로, whereas with verbs like "to get to" (이르다) or "to arrive" (도착하다), we use the particle 에.

Examples

Nouns without batchim	Nouns in ㄹ	Nouns with batchim
나무로	돌로	밥으로
컴퓨터로	발로	병으로
종이로	칼로	젓가락으로

This particle mainly performs the following functions:

1 It indicates means or instrument

I write a letter with a pen. ➡ 나는 펜으로 편지를 써요.
I go to Korea by plane. ➡ 나는 한국에 비행기로 가요.
I speak in Korean with a friend. ➡ 나는 친구와 한국말로 이야기해요.

2 It expresses meanings such as "as" or "in the capacity of."

I go to Korea as a scholarship student. ➡ 나는 장학생으로 한국에 가요.
I work as a tour guide. ➡ 나는 여행 가이드로 일해요.
I speak to you as a friend. ➡ 나는 친구로 당신에게 말해요.

3 It indicates direction or destination. In such a context, it is used to indicate the place toward which somebody or something is going.

I leave for Japan. ➡ 나는 일본으로 떠나요.
I go toward the school. ➡ 나는 학교로 가요.

4 Let's look here at some other common uses of the particle (으)로:

· being made of a material (made of wood, made of stone)
· with verbs indicating choice (I chose this article)
· with verbs expressing transformation (the tadpole turns into a frog)

Exercise 2   Translate into Korean.

1) I go to school by train.

2) I speak Chinese.

3) I leave for Japan.

연필
4) My friend writes with a pencil.

The honorific form, first part

Formal respect in conversation is of the utmost importance in Korean. If you do not show the right deference towards somebody, you run the risk of being perceived as offensive. Practically, we can categorize people into three groups: common people (사람), people who deserve our respect (분), and people who do not deserve our respect (놈, for example, a thief: 도둑)

We use honorific forms when the subject of the sentence is a 분 (because he or she is older than us, based on the person's role or position, or simply because we are not familiar with that person). This means that if I am speaking with a professor (분) about a boy (사람), I should **not** use the honorific form, whereas I should do so if I am referring to a professor while talking with a boy. A 분 can be a teacher (선생님), a university professor (교수님), a senior citizen (노인, 어르신), or someone we don't know very well.

Let's examine how to construct the honorific form case by case.

1. **First person**: we don't use the honorific form when talking about ourselves.

2. **Second person**: we use the honorific form if our conversation partner is a 분 and is also the subject of the sentence.

Professor, have you already eaten the apple? (We use the honorific form.)
Grandfather, what are you doing here? (We use the honorific form.)
Professor, my friend did not come to school (We do not use the honorific form.)

3. **Third person**: it is used not based on the status of the person we are talking to, but rather if the subject of the sentence is a 분.

The boss is in his office. (We use the honorific form.)
My father's computer is good. (We do not use the honorific form.)

The honorific form entails **different conjugations of verbs**. In some cases, one must also substitute nouns with their honorific forms and use honorific particles. In order to make a verb honorific, we must first check to see if the stem has a batchim. If the stem does not have a batchim, we simply put the suffix 시 between the stem and the declination of the verb. If the stem does have a batchim, we add the suffix 으시.

Nouns without batchim	Nouns with batchim
가다 ➡ 가시다	읽다 ➡ 읽으시다
보다 ➡ 보시다	덮다 ➡ 덮으시다

We must also consider some **exceptions**, which mirror the irregularities in conjugations for the semiformal register.

① Verbs whose stems end in ㄹ

In verbs with stems ending in ㄹ, the ㅅ is taken out (as discussed earlier, ㄹ always disappears when followed by ㄴ, ㅅ or ㅂ.)

만들다 ➡ 만드시다   놀다 ➡ 노시다   쓰다 ➡ 쓰시다

② Verbs whose stems end in ㄹ

Regular verbs with stems ending in ㄷ follow the general rule fo the honorific form. **Irregular** verbs, however, follow the construction of the semiformal register.

Regular verbs   닫다 ➡ 닫으시다   뺄다 ➡ 뺄으시다   뜯다 ➡ 뜯으시다

③ Verbs whose stems end in ㅂ

Regular verbs with stems ending in ㅂ follow the general rule for construction of the honorific form. If the verb is irregular, the ㅂ is dropped and an ㅜ is added in its place.

Regular verbs   뽑다 ➡ 뽑으시다   입다 ➡ 입으시다
Irregular verbs   춥다 ➡ 추우시다   곱다 ➡ 고우시다

❶ Verbs with stems ending in ㅅ

Regular verbs with ㅅ follow the normal construction of the honorific form. **Irregular** verbs lose their ㅅ and add a ㅡ to the root of the verb.

Regular verbs   웃다 ➡ 웃으시다   벗다 ➡ 벗으시다   빗다 ➡ 빗으시다
Irregular verbs   낫다 ➡ 나으시다   짓다 ➡ 지으시다   긋다 ➡ 그으시다

❷ Verbs with stems ending in ㅎ

Regular verbs with stems ending in ㅎ follow the general rule for the honorific form. If the verb is **irregular,** the ㅎ is dropped.

Regular verbs   좋다 ➡ 좋으시다   넣다 ➡ 넣으시다   낳다 ➡ 낳으시다
Irregular verbs   그렇다 ➡ 그러시다   어떻다 ➡ 어떠시다

After adding a suffix to indicate the honorific form, we can conjugate the verbs in the other level of speech we have already studied.

가셔요 — 가세요

가시

가십니다

가십니까

The semi-formal form is constructed with the suffix (으)시 and gains an ㅓ, even if the verb originally ends with a solar vowel.

The form -셔요 is technically correct, but nowadays –세요 form is used instead.

| Exercise 3 | Conjugate using the –세요 form. |

1) 보다   2) 치다   3) 돌다   4) 놀다   5) 듣다

6) 갚다   7) 벗다   8) 닫다   9) 하다   10) 놓다

Exercise 1   Conjugate the following verbs using the honorific form.

1) 오다/가다

_____

2) 주다/만들다

_____

3) 갚다/읽다

_____

4) 닫다/듣다

_____

5) 치다/가리다

_____

6) 많다/ 보다

_____

Exercise 2   Conjugate the following verbs using the ㅡ세요 form.

1) 떠나다/ 빼다

_____

2) 받다/주다

_____

3) 덮다/밟다

_____

4) 좁다/춥다

_____

5) 웃다/ 낫다

_____

6) 돕다/덥다

_____

Exercise 3   Translate into Korean.

1) with the pencil

_____

2) by the cellphone

_____

3) by plane

_____

4) with money

_____

5) with fire

_____

6) by bike

_____

Unit 13

성함이 어떻게 되세요?
What's your name?

The short negative form using 안 or 못
The honorific form, second part
The particles 에게서 and 한테서
The exhortative form in the formal level of speech (으) ㅂ시다

13

TEXT 1

13² 저는 술을 못 마셔요.
I can't drink alcohol.

저는 공부를 잘 못해요.
I don't study well.

같이 한국어를 공부합시다!
Let's study Korean together!

같이 영화를 봅시다!
Let's watch a movie together!

TEXT 2

13³ 선생님, 성함이 어떻게 되세요?
Sir, what is your name?

할머니께서는 댁에 계십니까?
Is your grandmother at home?

누구에게 편지를 쓰세요?
To whom are you writing (the letter)?

할아버지는 왜 진지를 안 드세요?
Why isn't grandfather eating?

The short negative form using 안 or 못

The short negative form in Korean can be easily constructed by putting the adverbs 안 or 못 before the verb. This negative form can indicate:

안 : Unwillingness to carry out an action
못: Impossibility of carrying out an action or inability to carry out an action

 **Examples using the adverb 안**

I don't sleep. ➡ 잠을 안 자요.
I don't read the newspaper. ➡ 신문을 안 읽어요.
I don't eat food. ➡ 나는 음식을 안 먹어요.

* With verbs ending with 하다 constructed with a direct object, the adverb comes between the direct object and the verb.

> I don't study. ➡ 공부를 안 해요.
> I don't think. ➡ 생각을 안 해요.

Don't forget that there are some verbs which end in 하다, but which are adjectival verbs. With these adjectival verbs, the adverb comes before the whole verb.

(It) is not clean.➡ 안 깨끗해요.   (It) is not tedious. ➡ 안 지루해요.
(He) is not clever.➡ 안 똑똑해요.   (I) am not tired.➡ 안 피곤해요.

Some verbs have their own negative forms:

알다 to know / 모르다 to not know 있다 to stay/ 없다 to not stay 이다 to be / 아니다 not to be

The negative form of a verb constructed with a Chinese term and 하다 can generally be obtained by using the character 불 (read as 부 when it comes before a ㅈ or ㄷ).
편하다 to be comfortable / 불편하다 to be uncomfortable 필요하다 to be necessary/ 불필요하다 to be unnecessary

---

Exercise 1   Translate into Korean.

1) I don't go to school.

2) I don't eat bread.

3) (My) friend does not leave for Japan.

4) I'm not coming home.

5) The professor does not read a book.

6) The teacher does not listen to the music.

7) Aren't you coming to my place today?

8) Don't you study in the library?

② The negative adverb 못 indicates the impossibility of carrying out an action due to reasons beyond the subject's control.

> When followed by a verb starting with a vowel, 못 is pronounced [몯]
> However, if it is followed by 하다, the ㅅ[ㄷ] is aspirated.
> 못 있어요
> [모디써요] 못해요 [모태요]

I can't eat. (because my belly aches) ➡ 밥을 못 먹어요.
I can't go to school. (because it is raining) ➡ 학교에 못 가요.
I can't buy the book. (because I have no money) ➡ 책을 못 사요.

* The verb 못하다 (written with no space) is transitive, and is used when somebody is not able to do something.
　　한국어를 못해요. I can't speak Korean. / 요리를 못해요. I can't cook.

Be careful with the following points: negative form expressed with 못.

a) it can't be used with the copula (the verb to be);
b) it can't be used with adjectival verbs. 못 (in the form -지 못하다, which we have not learned yet) can be used with adjectival verbs only when we wish to emphasize that the subject is not fulfilling the expectations of the speaker in relation to a certain quality or characteristic.
c) it is generally used with the verb "to know" and similar verbs (알다, 깨닫다, 지각하다, 인식하다, etc.), as it is beyond the control of the subject that he or she does not know, recognize, or understand something. This also applies to the expression "I did not hear", which is translated in Korean as 못 + 듣다. Likewise, "I did not understand'" that I was told, what was said to me) is translated in Korean as 못 + 알아듣다.

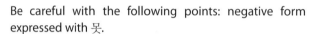

Exercise 2　Translate into Korean.

1) I can't go to school.

2) I can't eat bread.

3) Her friend can't leave.

4) He can't cook.

5) Can't you come to my place today?

6) Don't you speak French?

The honorific form, second part

In Korean, some verbs have their own honorific forms.

먹다 (to eat) ➡ 드시다/잡수시다
자다 (to sleep) ➡ 주무시다
아프다 (to feel bad) ➡ 편찮으시다

마시다 (to drink) ➡ 드시다/잡수시다
말하다 (to speak) ➡ 말씀하시다
죽다 (to die) ➡ 돌아가시다

Do you drink a coffee? 커피를 드세요?
Good night! 안녕히 주무세요!

Speak quiet. 천천히 말씀하세요.
Have a good time! 좋은 시간 보내세요!

The verb 있다 has two separate honorific forms. When used to express the meaning "to have", it becomes 있으시다, and for the meaning "to stay" it becomes 계시다. Its negative forms are 없으시다, meaning not to have, and 안 계시다, meaning not to be.

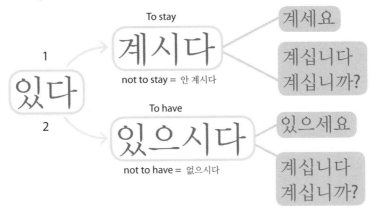

To stay
계시다
1
not to stay = 안 계시다

계세요

계십니다
계십니까?

있다

To have
2
있으시다
not to have = 없으시다

있으세요

계십니다
계십니까?

Exercise 3   Translate into Korean.

1) Professor, are you there?

2) Teacher, do you have a pen?

3) Grandmother is at the restaurant.

4) Grandfather is at the hospital.

Also, some nouns have an honorific form, which is used when the person we are addressing our respect.

1 Family members

아빠 (dad) ➡ 아버지 (or 아버님)
할아버지 (grandfather) ➡ 할아버님
아들 (son) ➡ 아드님
누나 (older sister of a boy) ➡ 누님
오빠 (older brother of a girl) ➡ 오라버니

엄마 (mom)➡ 어머니 (or 어머님)
할머니 (grandmother) ➡ 할머님
딸 (daughter) ➡ 따님
형 (older brother of a boy) ➡ 형님
부인 (wife) ➡ 사모님

2 Other nouns

밥 (meal) ➡ 진지
집 (house) ➡ 댁
생일 (birthday) ➡ 생신

말 (word) ➡ 말씀
나이 (age) ➡ 연세
이름 (name) ➡ 성함

Let's memorize some expressions:

이름이 뭐예요? ➡ (honorific form) 성함이 어떻게 되세요?

몇 살이에요? ➡ (honorific form) 연세가 어떻게 되세요?

The particles 에게서 and 한테서

The particles 에게서 and 한테서 are similar to the particles 에게 and 한테, but indicates origin or the person one receives or learns something from. They are often used with the verbs 받다 (to receive), 배우다 (to learn), 듣다 (to listen to), and 오다 (to come).

I receive a letter from a friend. ➡ 친구한테서 편지를 받아요.
I receive a present from my father. ➡ 아버지한테서 선물을 받아요.
Who are you learning English from? ➡ 영어를 누구한테서 배워요?

* In spoken Korean, 에게서 and 한테서 are often shortened to 에게 and 한테.

The exhortative form in the formal level of speech (으)ㅂ시다

In this unit we will introduce the exhortative form in the formal level of speech. This form follows the same main **exception** patterns of the verbs we have studied so far. It is not an honorific form, as the subject corresponds to the first person plural (we) and, as already noted, the honorific form cannot be used with the first person.

* The verb 그럽시다 is the exhortative form of the verb 그러다/그러하다 (means "to do"). It is not the exhortative form of 그렇다, which is an adjectival verb.

Let's go!

가다 ━ 갑시다   읽다 ━ 읽읍시다

Let's read!

① Verbs with stems ending in ㄹ
The ㄹ is dropped before the ㅂ.

만들다 ➡ 만듭시다   놀다 ➡ 놉시다

② Verbs with stems ending in ㄷ
Regular verbs with stems ending in ㄷ follow the general rule for formation of the honorific form. **Irregular** verbs behave as in the semiformal register.

regular verbs   닫다 ➡ 닫읍시다   뻗다 ➡ 뻗읍시다   뜯다 ➡ 뜯읍시다
irregular verbs   듣다 ➡ 들읍시다   묻다 ➡ 물읍시다   걷다 ➡ 걸읍시다

③ Verbs with stems ending in ㅂ
Regular verbs with stems ending in ㅂ follow the general rule for formation of the honorific form. **Irregular** verbs are generally adjectival verbs, and therefore cannot be used within the exhortative form.

regular verbs   뽑다 ➡ 뽑읍시다   입다 ➡ 입읍시다
irregular verbs   돕다 ➡ 도웁시다

④ Verbs with stems ending in ㅅ
Regular verbs with stems ending in ㅅ follow the general rule for formation of honorific form. For irregular verbs, it is necessary to drop the ㅅ and add an ㅡ to the root of the verb.

regular verbs   웃다 ➡ 웃읍시다   벗다 ➡ 벗읍시다
irregular verbs   긋다 ➡ 그읍시다

⑤ Verbs with stems ending in ㅎ
Regular verbs with stems ending in ㅎ follow the general rule for formation of the honorific form. **Irregular** verbs are adjectival verbs, and thus are not used in the exhortative form.

regular verbs   낳다 ➡ 낳읍시다

Exercise 1   Translate into Korean.

1) I receive a book from my sister.

_____

2) I receive a letter from the professor.

_____

3) He receives an email from a friend.

_____

4) She receives a present from her mother.

_____

5) The professor receives a letter from the student.

_____

Exercise 2   Translate into Korean.

1) My mother reads a newspaper.

_____

2) My grandmother eats well.

_____

3) My father sleeps at home.

_____

4) My grandfather isn't feeling well.

_____

5) My father speaks quietly.

_____

6) Mr. Kim goes to the library.

_____

Exercise 3   Dictation exercise: Listen and write.

13⁴

_____

_____

_____

_____

어제 친구랑 영화를 봤어요.
Yesterday I watched a movie with a friend.

- The honorific form, third part
- Imperative polite form (으)십시오
- Simple past tense –았/었/였–
- The particle (이)랑

 14

Vocabulary

귤 mandarin orange
데리고 가다 to accompany
드리다 to give*
딸기 strawberry
레몬 lemon
멜론 melon

바나나 banana
복숭아 peach
뵙다 to meet*
사장 boss
수박 watermelon
스테이크 steak

여쭈다 to ask*
연구실 laboratory
영화 movie
펭귄 penguin
포도 grape

TEXT 1

 저는 선생님께 선물을 드립니다.
I give a present to the teacher.

선생님께서 저에게 선물을 주십니다.
The teacher gives me a present.

내일 학교에 가십시오.
Go to school tomorrow.

교실에서 모자를 벗으십시오.
Take your hat off in the classroom.

TEXT 2

어제 무엇을 했어요?
What did you do yesterday?

어제 집에서 공부를 했어요.
Yesterday I studied at home.

어제 친구랑 영화를 봤어요.
Yesterday I watched a movie with a friend.

어제 피자랑 스파게티를 먹었어요.
Yesterday I ate pizza and spaghetti.

The honorific form, third part

Now let's look at three more aspects of the honorific form: **pronouns**, **humble verbs**, and **honorific particles**. With "humble personal pronouns" we mean 저 and 저희, which correspond to 나 and 우리, and are used to identify the first person singular or plural when speaking with a person who deserves respect, or in formal contexts.

> I talk to a teacher.   저는 선생님과 이야기합니다.
> I talk to my boss.   저는 사장님과 이야기합니다.

To these humble pronouns we add humble verbs, which are used instead of their regular counterparts in order to express respect.

만나다 (to meet) ➡ 뵙다
묻다 (to ask) ➡ 여쭈다
말하다 (to speak) ➡ 말씀드리다

데리고 가다 (to accompany) ➡ 모시다
주다 (to give) ➡ 드리다
인사하다 (to greet) ➡ 인사드리다

Be careful when using verb "**to give**": 1) When giving something to a friend, we use the verb 주다 2) If, instead, we give something to someone we owe respect to (분), we use 드리다. 3) On the other hand, if it is the person we owe respect to who gives us something, we use 주다 conjugated in the honorific form, which is 주시다.

1. 주다
나는 친구에게 돈을 줘요.
나는 병아리에게 밥을 줘요.
나는 화분에 물을 줘요.
2. 주시다
선생님은 돈을 주세요.
할머니는 전화를 주세요.
3. 드리다
저는 선생님에게 전화를 드려요.
저는 선생님에게 인사를 드려요.

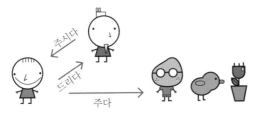

Exercise 1   Translate into Korean.

1) The teacher gives me a pen.

2) I give a newspaper to my father.

3) My father gives me 10,000 won.

4) I speak to the boss. (사장님)

141

When using honorific forms, many of the particles we have already learned must be replaced with honorific forms, as explained below.

1. 선생님이 가요.
➡ 선생님께서 가세요.

2. 선생님은 학교에 와요.
➡ 선생님께서는 학교에 오세요.

3. 선생님도 학교에 있어요.
➡ 선생님께서도 학교에 계세요.

4. 선생님에게 편지를 줘요.
➡ 선생님께 편지를 드려요.

5. 선생님에게서 편지를 받아요.
➡ 선생님께 편지를 받아요.

Below are some examples that show how these particles are used in complete sentences.

친구는 밥을 먹어요. ➡ 선생님께서는 진지를 드세요.
친구가 나한테 책을 줘요. ➡ 선생님께서 저에게 책을 주세요.
나는 친구한테서 책을 받아요. ➡ 저는 선생님께 책을 받아요.
친구도 학교에 있어요. ➡ 선생님께서도 학교에 계세요.

Exercise 2 Translate into Korean.

연구실
1) The teacher sleeps in the studio.

2) The teacher is also leaving for China.

3) I give my grandmother a bag.

4) The teacher has a computer.

Imperative polite form (으)십시오

To make a request to someone who deserves our respect, we use the **imperative polite** form. In this form, the verb stem is followed by the honorific suffix -(으)시 and the suffix - ㅂ시오.

Examples

1) 가다 ➡ 가시 + ㅂ시오 ➡ 가십시오 (Please go.)
2) 만들다 ➡ 만드시 + ㅂ시오 ➡ 만드십시오 (Please make it (Kindly make it.))
3) 듣다 ➡ 들으시 + ㅂ시오 ➡ 들으십시오 (Please listen to.)
4) 읽다 ➡ 읽으시 + ㅂ시오 ➡ 읽으십시오 (Please read.)

* In cases where honorific verbs exist (see p. 127), you must use them when using the imperative polite form.

1) 먹다 ➡ 드시 + ㅂ시오 ➡ 드십시오 (Please eat)
2) 자다 ➡ 주무시 + ㅂ시오 ➡ 주무십시오 (Please go to bed)

| Exercise 3 | Conjugate using the polite imperative form. |

1) 먹다   2) 치다   3) 자다   4) 주다   5) 묻다

6) 돌다   7) 닫다   8) 입다   9) 사다   10) 하다

Simple past tense −았/었/였−

To conjugate a verb in the past tense, first add the vowels ㅏ or ㅓ to the root of the verb, as is done when using the semi-formal register. The vowel is then followed by the suffix -ㅆ어요 (in the semiformal register) or -ㅆ습니다 (in the formal register).

1) 가다 ➡ 가 + ㅆ어요 ➡ 갔어요/갔습니다/갔습니까?
2) 만들다 ➡ 만들어 + ㅆ어요 ➡ 만들었어요/만들었습니다/만들었습니까?
3) 듣다 ➡ 들어 + ㅆ어요 ➡ 들었어요/들었습니다/들었습니까?
4) 읽다 ➡ 읽어 + ㅆ어요 ➡ 읽었어요/읽었습니다/읽었습니까?

Exercise 4   Conjugate in the simple past tense.

1) 먹다	2) 피다	3) 자다	4) 주다	5) 묻다
6) 돌다	7) 닫다	8) 입다	9) 그렇다	10) 하다

Let's try conjugating some verbs using both the past tense and the honorific form.

1) 가다 ➡ 가셨어요/가셨습니다/가셨습니까?
2) 만들다 ➡ 만드셨어요/만드셨습니다/만드셨습니까?
3) 듣다 ➡ 들으셨어요/들으셨습니다/들으셨습니까?
4) 읽다 ➡ 읽으셨어요/읽으셨습니다/읽으셨습니까?
5) 먹다 ➡ 잡수셨어요/잡수셨습니다/잡수셨습니까?

Exercise 5   Translate into Korean.

1) The teacher passed away.

2) Yesterday the teacher did not go to the university.

3) The professor ate a lot.

4) The boss gave two books.

The particle (이)랑

The particle (이)랑 can be translated as "with" or "together with," and can also be used as a **conjunction between two or more nouns**. In the case of nouns that have a batchim (including ㄹ), the particle requires the addition of an 이. (이)랑 is mainly used in spoken Korean.

Examples

Nouns without batchim	Nouns with batchim
나 (I) ➡ 나랑	책 (book) ➡ 책이랑
친구 (friend) ➡ 친구랑	밥 (tree) ➡ 밥이랑
엽서 (postcard) ➡ 엽서랑	펭귄 (penguin) ➡ 펭귄이랑

* When this particle denotes accompaniment, it can be followed by the adverbs 함께 or 같이 (together).

나랑 같이 (with me)
선생님이랑 함께 (with the teacher)

This particle is also used to coordinate nouns, and is often used when ordering food.

1) 친구랑 나랑 (My friend and me)
2) 에스프레소랑 아메리카노랑 카푸치노를 주세요.

Exercise 6   Translate into Korean using the particle (이)랑.

1) Bananas and strawberries

2) Watermelons and tangerines

3) Melons and lemons

4) Grapes and peaches

Exercise 1   Replace the particle with its honorific form.

1) 선생님은

_____

2) 교수님이

_____

3) 교수님에게

_____

4) 선생님한테서

_____

5) 할머니가

_____

6) 사장님에게

_____

Exercise 2   Translate the following sentences using honorific forms.

1) The professor goes to Seoul.

_____

2) Tomorrow his father comes too.

_____

3) The boss gives us presents.

_____

4) The writer and the professor have lunch.

_____

5) (My) grandfather is not at home.

_____

6) (My) grandfather drinks water.

_____

Exercise 3   Conjugate the following verbs in the simple past form.

1) 가다

_____

2) 보다

_____

3) 주다

_____

4) 먹다

_____

5) 죽다

_____

6) 자다

_____

APPENDIX

Verbs: summary of the conjugations

Verb	ㅂ/습니다	아/어/여요	(으)ㅂ시다	(으)세요	았/었/였어요	(으)셨어요
가르다 to divide	가릅니다	갈라요	가릅시다	가르세요	갈랐어요	가르셨어요
갈다 to sharpen	갑니다	갈아요	갑시다	가세요	갈았어요	가셨어요
걷다 to walk	걷습니다	걸어요	걸읍시다	걸으세요	걸었어요	걸으셨어요
고맙다 to be grateful	고맙습니다	고마워요	-	-	고마웠어요	-
곱다 to be beautiful	곱습니다	고와요	-	고우세요	고왔어요	고우셨어요
괜찮다 to be fine	괜찮습니다	괜찮아요	-	괜찮으세요	괜찮았어요	괜찮으셨어요
그렇다 to be like that	그렇습니다	그래요	-	그러세요	그랬어요	그러셨어요
긋다 to mark	긋습니다	그어요	그읍시다	그으세요	그었어요	그으셨어요
깎다 to peel	깎습니다	깎아요	깎읍시다	깎으세요	깎았어요	깎으셨어요
끄다 to switch off	끕니다	꺼요	끕시다	끄세요	껐어요	끄셨어요
낫다 to be better	낫습니다	나아요	-	나으세요	나았어요	나으셨어요
낳다 to give birth	낳습니다	낳아요	낳읍시다	낳으세요	낳았어요	낳으셨어요
넓다 to be wide	넓습니다	넓어요	-	넓으세요	넓었어요	넓으셨어요
노랗다 to be yellow	노랗습니다	노래요	-	노라세요	노랬어요	노라셨어요
누르다 to push	누릅니다	눌러요	누릅시다	누르세요	눌렀어요	누르셨어요
다루다 to deal	다룹니다	다뤄요	다룹시다	다루세요	다루었어요	다루셨어요
다르다 to be different	다릅니다	달라요	-	다르세요	달랐어요	다르셨어요
닫다 to close	닫습니다	닫아요	닫읍시다	닫으세요	닫았어요	닫으셨어요
달리다 to run	달립니다	달려요	달립시다	달리세요	달렸어요	달리셨어요
덥다 to be warm	덥습니다	더워요	-	더우세요	더웠어요	더우셨어요
덮다 to cover	덮습니다	덮어요	덮읍시다	덮으세요	덮었어요	덮으셨어요
돌다 to turn	돕니다	돌아요	돕시다	도세요	돌았어요	도셨어요
돕다 to help	돕습니다	도와요	도웁시다	도우세요	도왔어요	도우셨어요

Verb	ㅂ/습니다	아/어/여요	(으)ㅂ시다	(으)세요	았/었/였어요	(으)셨어요
두르다 to put around	두릅니다	둘러요	두릅시다	두르세요	둘렀어요	두르셨어요
듣다 to listen	듣습니다	들어요	들읍시다	들으세요	들었어요	들으셨어요
따르다 to follow	따릅니다	따라요	따릅시다	따르세요	따랐어요	따르셨어요
뜯다 to open (a box)	뜯습니다	뜯어요	뜯읍시다	뜯으세요	뜯었어요	뜯으셨어요
마르다 to be dry	마릅니다	말라요	-	마르세요	말랐어요	마르셨어요
많다 to be numerous	많습니다	많아요	-	많으세요	많았어요	많으셨어요
맵다 to be spicy	맵습니다	매워요	-	매우세요	매웠어요	매우셨어요
모르다 not to know	모릅니다	몰라요	-	모르세요	몰랐어요	모르셨어요
몰다 to drive	몹니다	몰아요	-	모세요	몰았어요	모셨어요
묻다 to ask	묻습니다	물어요	물읍시다	물으세요	물었어요	물으셨어요
묻다 to bury	묻습니다	묻어요	묻읍시다	묻으세요	묻었어요	묻으셨어요
믿다 to believe	믿습니다	믿어요	믿읍시다	믿으세요	믿었어요	믿으셨어요
밉다 to be obnoxious	밉습니다	미워요	-	미우세요	미웠어요	미우셨어요
반갑다 to be glad	반갑습니다	반가워요	-	반가우세요	반가웠어요	반가우셨어요
받다 to receive	받습니다	받아요	받읍시다	받으세요	받았어요	받으셨어요
벗다 to undress	벗습니다	벗어요	벗읍시다	벗으세요	벗었어요	벗으셨어요
붓다 to pour	붓습니다	부어요	-	부으세요	부었어요	부으셨어요
비웃다 to mock	비웃습니다	비웃어요	비웃읍시다	비웃으세요	비웃었어요	비웃으셨어요
빗다 to comb	빗습니다	빗어요	빗읍시다	빗으세요	빗었어요	빗으셨어요
빠르다 to be fast	빠릅니다	빨라요	-	빠르세요	빨랐어요	빠르셨어요
빨갛다 to be red	빨갛습니다	빨개요	-	빨가세요	빨갰어요	빨가셨어요
빨다 to wash	빱니다	빨아요	빱시다	빠세요	빨았어요	빠셨어요
빼앗다 to deduct	빼앗습니다	빼앗아요	빼앗읍시다	빼앗으세요	빼앗았어요	빼앗으셨어요

Verbs: summary of the conjugations

Verb	ㅂ/습니다	아/어/여요	(으)ㅂ시다	(으)세요	았/었/였어요	(으)셨어요
세다 to be strong	셉니다	세요	-	세세요	셌어요	세셨어요
솟다 to gush	솟습니다	솟아요	-	솟으세요	솟았어요	솟으셨어요
싣다 to load	싣습니다	실어요	실읍시다	실으세요	실었어요	실으셨어요
쏟다 to pour out	쏟습니다	쏟아요	쏟읍시다	쏟으세요	쏟았어요	쏟으셨어요
씻다 to wash	씻습니다	씻어요	씻읍시다	씻으세요	씻었어요	씻으셨어요
아름답다 to be beautiful	아름답습니다	아름다워요	-	아름다우세요	아름다웠어요	아름다우셨어요
업다 to shoulder (a burden)	업습니다	업어요	업읍시다	업으세요	업었어요	업으셨어요
입다 to wear	입습니다	입어요	입읍시다	입으세요	입었어요	입으셨어요
잇다 to follow	잇습니다	이어요	이읍시다	이으세요	이었어요	이으셨어요
좁다 to be narrow	좁습니다	좁아요	-	좁으세요	좁았어요	좁으셨어요
좋다 to be good	좋습니다	좋아요	-	좋으세요	좋았어요	좋으셨어요
지르다 to shout	지릅니다	질러요	지릅시다	지르세요	질렀어요	지르셨어요
짓다 to make	짓습니다	지어요	지읍시다	지으세요	지었어요	지으셨어요
춥다 to be cold	춥습니다	추워요	-	추우세요	추웠어요	추우셨어요
치르다 to support	치릅니다	치러요	치릅시다	치르세요	치렀어요	치르셨어요
파랗다 to be blue	파랗습니다	파래요	-	파라세요	파랬어요	파라셨어요
하다 to do	합니다	해요	합시다	하세요	했어요	하셨어요
하얗다 to be white	하얗습니다	하얘요	-	하야세요	하얬어요	하야셨어요

When to use the particles 이/가 and 은/는

Here we will explain in greater depth the usage of these two particles.

1 We use the particle 이/가 when . . .

It stresses (emphasizes) the subject.

> It is going to rain/It's raining. (비) ➡ 비가 와요.
> It is going to snow/It's snowing. (눈) ➡눈이 와요.

It modifies subject.
It is often used with adjectival verbs (and often refers to inanimate subjects).

> The house is small. ➡ 집이 좁아요.
> The weather is cold. ➡날씨가 추워요.
> The classroom is noisy. ➡교실이 시끄러워요.

It is used in questions together with interrogative pronouns, such as 누가, 무엇이 (뭐가), 어디 and 언제.

> Who came? A friend came. ➡ 누가 왔어요? 친구가 왔어요.
> Who ate the pizza? I ate it. ➡누가 피자를 먹었어요? 내가 먹었어요.

In both examples, the particle emphasizes that a specific person carried out the action.

It stresses (emphasizes) the subject in subordinate clauses.

> The dog that I saw . . . (내가 본 그 개는 . . .)
> I know that he has arrived. (나는 그 사람이 왔다는 것을 알아요.)

It emphasizes (stresses) new information.
When a new topic is introduced for the first time, we use 이/가.
When it is already known to our conversation partner, we use 은/는.

> There is a house there. 거기엔 집이 있어요.
> That house is located by the seaside. 그집은 바닷가에 있어요.

* The particle 은/는 may also be used in responses to questions. As shown below, the questions were formed using 이/가.

이름이 뭐예요? 제 이름은 안드레아예요.
고향 (hometown) 이 어디예요? 제 고향은 로마예요.
전공 (major) 이 뭐예요? 전공은 한국학 (Korean studies)이에요.

2 We use the particle 은/는 when...

We wish to highlight the topic of the sentence.
It can be translated as "concerning," "regarding," or "as for." It can be applied to any element in the discourse; it is not limited to the subject.

김은정은 한국 사람이에요. 회사원이에요. 36살이에요.
(Kim Eunjeong is Korean. She is an employee. She is thirty-six years old.)
(The topic, Kim Eunjeong is the same for all three sentences).

It emphasizes a contrast or a comparison.
The particle 은/는 can be used to emphasize a contrast or a comparison. We can therefore find it in contrasting clauses, where it is often introduced by 하지만, 그렇지만, or 그런데 (but, however), and in negative clauses (where it stresses the element being denied). In some contexts, it can be translated as "instead."

나는 이탈리아 사람입니다. 그 사람은 중국 사람이에요.
I am Italian. He is Chinese.
나는 이것을 하지만 그 사람은 다른 것을 합니다.
I do this, but he does that instead.
작년에는 바다에 갔어요. 하지만 올해는 안 갔어요.
Last year I went to the sea. However, this year I didn't.
친구는 집에 없어요.
(My) friend is not at home.
이것은 안 먹어요!
I won't eat that!

In other contexts, it can be used to change the topic of the sentence.

실례합니다. 김치찌개가 얼마예요? 10,000원입니다.	Excuse me, how much is the kimchi jjigae? It is 10,000 won.

그럼, 된장찌개는 얼마예요?   And how about the doenjang jjigae?
8,000원입니다.   It is 8,000 won.
그럼 볶음밥은요?   And how about the fried rice?

* In the last example, note that the particle 은/는 is directly followed by the suffix -요, which indicates the semiformal conversational register. Here, the particle is used in the sense, "how about (this other dish) instead"?

친구는요? And what about your friend?
어머님은요? What about your mother?

It is generally used in affirmative noun phrases.

I am Korean. ➡ 나는 한국 사람이에요.
He is a singer. ➡ 그 사람은 가수예요.

③ We use both particles when...

Some constructions require both particles. For example, the negative noun phrase (see page 66) requires both. In this case, we express the subject using 은/는, while we express the nominal predicate with 이/가.

I am Korean. ➡ 나는 한국 사람이에요.
He is a singer. ➡ 그 사람은 가수예요.

As discussed earlier, other constructions (e.g. possession) also require the use of both particles (**see pages 78-79**). Additionally, both particles can be used to express "I like/I don't like something."

나는 김치가 좋아요. As for me, kimchi is good. (I like kimchi.)
나는 김치가 싫어요. As for me, kimchi is not tasty. (I don't like kimchi.)

④ We can use either of the two particles when

In many circumstances, a sentence can be grammatically correct by using both 은/는 and 이/가. However, the use of one or the other can slightly modify the meaning, as you can see in the following examples:

a. Who went home? ➡ 안드레아가 집에 갔어요.

    b. What did Andrea do? ➡ 안드레아는 집에 갔어요.

Both sentences are correct, but the first emphasizes that it was Andrea, and not someone else, who performed the action, while the second stresses that Andrea went home.

    a. 무궁화는 대한민국의 나라꽃이에요.
    b. 무궁화가 대한민국의 나라꽃예요. The Rose of Sharon is the Korean national flower.

In the first case the sentence only describes the subject (the Rose of Sharon), while in the second it provides an answer to the question "What is the Korean national flower?"

    a. 로마는 이탈리아의 수도입니다.
    b. 로마가 이탈리아의 수도입니다. (Rome is the capital of Italy.)

In the first sentence, while describing Rome, we point out that it is the capital of Italy. In the second sentence, we are answering the question "What is the capital of Italy?"

How to write an email

In this section of the book, we will look at the conventions of email writing in Korean. Included in the text below are some grammatical forms you haven't learned yet: oftentimes, these are standard forms used in emails which a student is able to understand fully only in the more advanced stages of study. Let's start with an example of an email:

받는 사람 Recipient	ahnsonjae@korean.co.kr
보내는 사람 Sender	andrea@korean.co.kr
제목 Subject	

💾 첨부파일 Attachment ✉️→ 보내기 Send

Good morning Professor! This is Andrea. I hope everything is fine with you. It is very hot lately. How is your health? I apologize for not having contacted you. Everything is fine with me.	선생님 안녕하세요? 안드레아입니다. *Meanwhile* 그동안 잘 지내셨어요? *Lately it is hot, but health* 요즘 날씨가 많이 더운데 건강은 어떠세요? *I couldn't contact you* 자주 연락드리지 못해서 죄송합니다. 저는 잘 지내고 있습니다.	**1** Greetings, introduction, some reference to the weather conditions, apologies and updates
I am writing, because next week I'm coming back to Korea and I would like to meet you. Do you have any time on Monday? I would like to eat together and talk with you.	*actually, the fact is that…* 다름이 아니라 다음 주에 다시 한국으로 *I go back, but I would like to meet* 돌아가는데 선생님을 뵙고 싶습니다. 월요일에 시간 있으세요? *I would like (I wish I)* 같이 식사하고 이야기도 하고 싶습니다.	**2** purpose of the email
I am waiting for your reply. I wish you a good day.	*Reply I will wait A good day* 그럼 답장 기다리겠습니다 좋은 하루 *I hope* 되시기 바랍니다.	**3** closing
Thank you.	감사합니다. 안드레아 드림	**4** signature

In this example email, note that the email is characterized by 1) an introduction 2) a section that explains why you are writing 3) final greetings and 4) a signature. Let's take into account two kinds of emails: those addressed to somebody we are not familiar with, and those addressed to somebody with whom we are better acquainted.

Example of an email sent to somebody we are not familiar with

Recipient

선생님 (교수님, 사장님, 선배님, etc.),
*We can use the particles 에게 or 께 after the name or title of the recipient

Greetings

안녕하십니까?

Introduction

My name is Andrea. 저는 안드레아라고 합니다.
I'm Andrea and I study at Rome University. 저는 로마 대학교에서 공부하는 안드레아라고 합니다.
My name is Andrea and I come from Italy. 저는 이탈리아에서 온 안드레아라고 합니다.
I am Andrea and I live in Venice. 저는 베네치아에 사는 안드레아라고 합니다.
I am glad to meet you. 만나서 반갑습니다.
It was a pleasure to meet you. 이렇게 알게 되어서 기쁩니다.
Allow me to introduce myself by email. 이메일로 먼저 인사드립니다.
I am sorry to contact you so suddenly. 갑자기 연락을 드려서 죄송합니다.

Purpose of the email

The reason I am writing is 제가 이메일을 쓰는 이유는 . . . 입니다.
The fact is . . . 다름이 아니라 . . .
I am writing because I have something I need to tell you. 드릴 말씀이 있어서 이렇게 이메일을 보냅니다.
I am writing because I need to ask you a question. 질문이 있어서 이렇게 이메일을 보냅니다.
I am writing because there is something I would like to ask. 궁금한 것이 있어서 이렇게 이메일을 보냅니다.
I am writing because I need to ask you a favour. 부탁이 있어서 이렇게 이메일을 보냅니다.

Closing

Thank you for reading my email. 제 이메일을 읽어 주셔서 감사합니다.

I ask that you kindly to reply as soon as possible. 빠른 답변 기다리겠습니다.
I will contact you again. 다음에 다시 연락 드리겠습니다.
I wish you a good day. 좋은 하루 되시기 바랍니다.
I wish you a good weekend. 좋은 주말 되시기 바랍니다.
Please feel free to contact me whenever you like. 언제든지 연락주시기 바랍니다.
Thank you. 감사합니다.
My message ends here. 이상입니다.

Signature
The name of the sender can be followed by 드림/올림.

Example of an email to someone with whom you are familiar

Greetings and introduction
Hello! It's Andrea here. 안녕하십니까 (안녕하세요)? 안드레아입니다 (안드레아예요).
(Title) How are you?. This is Andrea. 선생님/사장님/선배/언니, 안녕하세요? 안드레아입니다.
Thanks for your reply. 답변 감사합니다.
Thanks for the email. 보내주신 메일 잘 받았습니다.
Thanks for sending the file. 보내주신 파일 잘 받았습니다.

Remarks about the weather
It's gotten nice and warm lately. 요즘 날씨가 참 따뜻합니다.
The weather is very hot lately. 요즘 날씨가 많이 덥습니다.
It is really chilly. 날씨가 많이 쌀쌀합니다.
The temperature has dropped a lot lately. 날씨가 많이 추워졌습니다.
Time goes by quickly. 시간이 참 빨리 지나갑니다.
It is already June. 벌써 6월입니다.

Polite questions
How are you? (How have you been since the last time we met?) 그동안 잘 지내셨어요?
How have you been lately? 요즘 어떻게 지내세요?
Have you been very busy lately? 요즘 많이 바쁘시죠?
How is your health? 건강은 어떠세요?

Purpose of the email
The reason I am writing is 제가 이메일을 쓰는 이유는 ... 입니다.
The fact is ... 다름이 아니라 ...
Actually ... 실은 ...

I am writing because I want to tell you something. 드릴 말씀이 있어서 이렇게 이메일을 보냅니다.

I am writing because I have a question to ask you. 질문이 있어서 이렇게 이메일을 보냅니다.

I am writing because there is something I would like to know. 궁금한 것이 있어서 이렇게 이메일을 보냅니다.

I am writing because I need to ask you a favour. 부탁이 있어서 이렇게 이메일을 보냅니다.

Closing

I will stop here. 이만 줄이겠습니다.

I wish you good health. 항상 건강하세요.

It is very cold. Take good care of yourself. 날씨가 많이 춥습니다. 감기 조심하세요.

I will contact you again. 또 연락 드리겠습니다.

I will write again soon. 조만간 다시 연락 드리겠습니다.

I wish you a good day. 좋은 하루 보내시기 바랍니다.

I am waiting for your reply. 답장 기다릴게요.

Signature

Name of the sender followed by 드림/올림 (if you have much respect for the recipient), or by 씀/(이)가.

Let's try writing an email addressed to our teacher.

What do we call each other inside our family

1) 할아버지/할머니 - grandfather/grandmother
2) 아버지/어머니 - father/mother
3) 오빠 - elder brother of a woman
4) 형 - elder brother of a man
5) 동생 - younger brother/sister of a man/woman
6) 언니 - elder sister of a woman
7) 누나 - elder sister of a man
8) 고모 - father's sister (aunt)
9) 이모 - mother's sister (aunt)
10) 삼촌 - father's brother (uncle)
11) 삼촌 - mother's brother (uncle)

What do we call each other inside our family

Some of the words from the list above can also be used to address people to whom we are not related. These words show courtesy and respect.

1) 할아버지 Grandfather/ 할머니 Grandmother – These can be used when a child/young person talks to a senior person.
2) 오빠/형 Older brother/언니/누나 Older sister - These can be used towards older people with whom we have some degree of familiarity/intimacy (friends in general, or university classmates)
3) 언니 Older sister/ 이모 Aunt - These are two polite ways to address an oder woman. They are used, for example, by the owner of a restaurant or shop with customers.)

In Korean, it can often be difficult to determine the best way to address the person one is talking to. However, it is not appropriate to overuse the second-person personal pronoun unless the person is someone we are very familiar with. In a formal conversation, we can use the title or the first name, followed by -씨/-님. In other cases we can use:
Sir 아저씨 Madam 아주머니 - You can use these titles to address a mature person in a less distinct context (restaurant, market). If we see a man on campus who looks like a teacher, it is better to avoid addressing him as such. Moreover, it can easily be offensive to women of a certain social status (professional women) to be addressed this way. 아저씨 is also used (as a joke) by young people with their peers (for example, when they

are attempting to seem conservative), in a university environment, or with older friends who have already served in the army.

총각 Bachelor/아가씨 Unmarried woman - These are used by senior persons to address younger persons, who are presumably unmarried.

학생 Student - This term is used by mature persons or by seniors when talking with school-age children or young people .

When none of these words seems correct for the circumstances, one can also use the neutral 거기요 and 저기요.

Unit 2

〈p. 20〉
Exercise 7
1) 가다 - 가(X) 2) 밝다 - 밝(O) 3) 뵙다 - 뵙(O) 4) 듣기 - 듣(O) 5) 크다 - 크(X) 6) 먹다 - 먹(O) 7) 읽다 - 읽(O) 8) 옮다 - 옮(O) 9) 타다 - 타(X) 10) 돌다 - 돌(O)

Unit 3

〈p. 30〉
Exercise 3
1) 가슴을[가스믈] 2) 돌아[도라] 3) 마음이[마으미] 4) 서울에[서우레] 5) 할아버님이[하라버니미] 6) 쌀이[싸리] 7) 흙을[흘글] 8) 밟을[발블] 9) 눈이[누니] 10) 인어공주[이너공주]

〈p. 30〉
Exercise 4
1) 각하[가카] 2) 빻다[빠타] 3) 놓지[노치] 4) 박해[바캐] 5) 넣죠[너쵸] 6) 낳다[나타] 7) 법하다[버파다] 8) 굽히다[구피다] 9) 좋대요[조태요] 10) 국학[구칵]

〈p. 32〉
Exercise 5
1) agi 2) geonbae 3) kwiji 4) junbi 5) seolbi 6) gogi 7) hangugeo 8) gongal 9) abi 10) eobu 11) bangji 12) gangguk 13) abeoji 14) nongbu 15) jiog'i 16) jigu 17) babo 18) bulgeo 19) gamgi 20) munje

〈p. 33〉
Exercise 6
1) 갑[갑] 2) 잎[입] 3) 옷[온] 4) 빛[빋] 5) 부엌[부억] 6)국[국] 7) 멋[먿] 8) 숲[숩] 9) 부엌에[부어케] 10) 및[믿]

〈p. 35〉
Execise 7
1) 칩니다[침니다] 2) 갚네요[갑네요 ->감네요] 3) 밥만[밤만] 4) 빛만[빋만 -> 빈만] 5) 국물[궁물] 6) 국립[궁립 -> 궁닙] 7) 독립[동립 -> 동닙] 8)

묻네요[문네요] 9) 볶는다[복는다 -> 봉는다] 10) 합리화[함니화] 11) 악몽[앙몽] 12) 좁네[좀네] 13) 갚네[갑네 -> 감네] 14) 디귿만[디근만] 15) 덫만[덛만 -> 던만] 16) 씁니다[씀니다] 17) 봅니다[봄니다] 18) 맞네[맏네 -> 만네] 19) 맛만[맏만 -> 만만] 20) 먹는다[멍는다]

〈p. 36〉
Execise 8
1) 먹지[먹찌] 2) 국자[국짜] 3) 뜨겁군[뜨겁꾼] 4) 집도[집또] 5) 밥도[밥또] 6) 맥주[맥쭈] 7) 각지다[각찌다] 8) 법적[법쩍] 9) 먹보[먹뽀] 10) 볶다[복따] 11) 악단[악딴] 12) 학자[학짜] 13) 걷자[걷짜] 14) 합법[합뻡] 15) 듣다[듣따]

〈p. 37〉
Execise 9
1) 신라[실라] 2) 심리[심니] 3) 감리[감니] 4) 발달[발딸] 5) 전래[절래] 6) 결심[결씸] 7)법률[범뉼] 8) 침략[침냑] 9) 결사[결싸] 10) 벌낫[벌란] 11) 길조[길쪼] 12) 망라[망나] 13) 결정[결쩡] 14) 갈등[갈뜽] 15) 필사[필싸]

〈p. 38〉
Execise 10
1) 값을[갑슬] 2) 몫[목] 3) 넓지[널찌] 4) 읊다[읍따] 5) 흙덩어리[흑떵어리] 6) 붉다[북따] 7) 여덟시[여덜씨] 8) 밟던[밥떤] 9) 많죠[만쵸] 10) 않습니다[안씀니다]

〈p. 44〉
Execise 1
쥐, 말, 의자, 꽃가게, 의사, 사투리

Exercise 2
1) 좋게[조케] 2) 같이[가치] 3) 막히게[마키게] 4) 국립[궁닙] 5) 내과[내꽈] 6) 읽다[익따] 7)법학[버팍] 8) 압박[압빡] 9) 빗살[비쌀] 10) 신라[실라] 11) 전래[절래] 12) 침략[침냑] 13) 한자[한짜] 14) 학교[학꾜] 15) 닳다[달따] 16) 여권[여꿘] 17) 성격[성껵] 18) 문법[문뻡]

Unit 4

⟨p. 47⟩
Exercise 1
1) 값은 2) 많은 3) 친구는 4) 돈은 5) 나무는 6) 돌은 7) 쌀은 8) 집은 9) 사랑은 10) 도서관은

⟨p. 48⟩
Exercise 2
1) 봅니다 2) 옵니다 3) 칩니다 4) 씁니다 5) 나쁩니다 6) 꿉니다 7) 춥니다 8) 탑니다 9) 컵니다 10) 예쁩니다

⟨p. 49⟩
Exercise 3
1) 덮습니다 2) 밉습니다 3) 덥습니다 4) 춥습니다 5) 감습니다 6) 괜찮습니다 7) 막습니다 8) 그렇습니다 9) 듣습니다 10) 맵습니다

Exercise 4
1) 만듭니다 2) 붑니다 3) 듭니다 4) 멉니다 5) 삽니다 6) 굽니다 7) 밉니다 8) 넙니다 9) 꿉니다 10) 빕니다

⟨p. 50⟩
Exercise 5
1) 잡니까? 2) 돕니까? 3) 떠납니까? 4) 맵습니까? 5) 삽니까? 6) 엽니까?

⟨p. 51⟩
Exercise 6
1) 계란입니까? 2) 의자입니까? 3) 책입니까? 4) 선생님입니까? 5) 말입니까? 6) 나무입니까?

⟨p. 52⟩
Exercise 1
1) 칩니다 2) 받습니다 3) 굽니다 4) 마십니다 5) 낳습니다 6) 밉니다 7) 씁니다 8) 짓습니다 9) 빱니다

Exercise 2
1) 저는 친구입니다. 2) 저는 고양이입니다. 3) 저는 매미입니다 4) 사자입니까? 5) 개구리입니까? 6) 초콜릿입니까? 7) 네, 컴퓨터입니다. 8) 네, 아이입니다. 9) 네, 오이입니다.

Exercise3
1) 공부합니까? 2) 먹습니다 3) 나는 학생입니다 4) 읽습니다 5) 벌레입니다 6) 바지입니다 7) 쥐입니다 8) 사투리입니다 9)나무입니까?

Unit 5

⟨p. 56⟩
Exercise 1
1) 이 말 2) 이 쥐 3) 저(/그) 나무 4) 저(/그) 의자 5) 저(/그) 밤 6 저(/그) 고양이

Exercise 2
1) 친구의 학교 2) 의사의 휴대폰 3) 학생의 어머니 4) 아버지의 가구 5) 선생님의 책 6)딸의 책상

⟨p. 60⟩
Exercise 3
1)저것은 누구의 탈입니까? 2)저것은 누구의 의자입니까? 3) 이 의사는 누구입니까? 4) 이 사람은 누구입니까?
 5) 저 사람은 안드레아 씨입니다. 6) 이것은 누구의 휴대폰입니까? 7) 이것은 누구의 공입니까? 8) 이 학생은 누구입니까?

⟨p. 61⟩
Exercise 4
1) 이것은 무엇입니까? / 이것은 드라이기입니다. 2) 이것은 무엇입니까? / 이것은 충전기입니다. 3) 이것은 무엇입니까? / 이것은 이어폰입니다. 4) 이것은 무엇입니까? / 이것은 선풍기입니다. 5) 저것은 무엇입니까? / 저것은 휴대폰입니다. 6) 저것은 무엇입니까? / 저것은 전기밥솥입니다. 7) 저것은 무엇입니까? / 저것은 사진기입니다. 8) 저것은 무엇입니까? / 저것은 냉장고입니다.

⟨p. 62⟩
Exercise 1
1) 내 친구의 휴대폰 2) 어머니의 냉장고 3) 아이의 고양이 4) 선생님의 공책 5) 여동생의 가방/언니의 가방 6) 꽃의 가시

Execise 2
1) 이것은 가방입니다. 2) 이 사람은 친구입니다.
3) 이것은 바지입니다. 4) 이 사람은 어머니입니다. 5) 저것은 꽃입니다. 6) 저 사람은 교수입니다.

Execise 3
1) 이것은 선생님의 볼펜입니다.
2) 그것은 어머니의 컴퓨터입니다.
3) 저것은 의사의 의자입니다.

Unit 6

⟨p. 65⟩
Execise 1
1) 값이 2) 몫이 3) 친구가 4) 돈이 5) 나무가 6) 마차가 7) 기분이 8) 집이 9) 사랑이 10) 학교가

⟨p. 67⟩
Execise 2
1) 저는 일본 사람이 아닙니다. 2) 이 집은 당신의 친구의 집이 아닙니까? 3) 이것은 컴퓨터가 아닙니다. 4) 이것은 제 개(강아지)가 아닙니다. 5) 이 사람은 그 사람의 친구가 아닙니까? 6) 이것은 한국어 책이 아닙니다.

Execise 3
1) 이것은 기차입니까? / 아니요, 기차가 아닙니다. 배입니다. 2) 이것은 자동차입니까? / 아니요, 자동차가 아닙니다. 기차입니다. 3) 이것은 자전거입니까? / 아니요, 자전거가 아닙니다. 자동차입니다. 4) 이것은 비행기입니까? / 아니요, 비행기가 아닙니다. 자전거입니다. 5) 이것은 마차입니까? / 아니요, 마차가 아닙니다. 비행기입니다. 6) 이것은 버스입니까? / 아니요, 버스가 아닙니다. 마차입니다. 7) 이것은 탱크입니까? / 아니요, 탱크가 아닙니다. 버스입니다. 8) 이것은 배입니까? / 아니요, 배가 아닙니다. 탱크입니다.

⟨p. 70⟩
Execise 1
1) 는 2) 는, 이 3) 은, 이 4) 는, 가 5) 은, 가 6) 는

Execise 2
1) 저는 한국 사람이 아닙니다. 2) 저것은 그녀의 자동차가 아닙니다. 3) 선생님은 중국인이 아닙니다. 4) 저것은 코미디 영화가 아닙니다. 5) 이것은 내 가방이 아닙니다. 6) 저것은 제 볼펜이 아닙니다. 7) 무슨 말입니까? 8) 어떤 영화를 좋아합니까? 9) 이 두 개 스웨터 중에서 어떤/어느 것을 좋아합니까? 10) 어느 나라 사람입니까? 11) 당신 친구는 어떤 사람입니까? 12) 오늘은 무슨 요일입니까?

Unit 7

⟨p. 73⟩
Execise 1
1) 학교에 2) 중국에 3) 도시에 4) 미국에 5) 한국에 6) 스페인에 7) 일본에 8) 기숙사에 9) 상자에 10) 브라질에 11) 온라인에 12) 그 나라에 13) 봉투에 14) 인터넷에 15) 이탈리아에 16) 이 건물에

⟨p. 74⟩
Execise 2
1) 시장에 갑니다. 2) 중국에 갑니다. 3) 도시에 갑니다. 4) 외국에 갑니다. 5) 한국에 갑니다. 6) 산에 갑니다. 7) 바다에 갑니다. 8) 화성에 갑니다.

⟨p. 75⟩
Execise 3
1) 나는 시장에 있습니다. 2) 친구는 외국에 있습니다. 3) 학생은 기숙사에 있습니다. 4) 어머니는 집에 있습니다.

⟨p. 77⟩
Execise 4
1) 컴퓨터가 의자 위에 있습니다. / 컴퓨터는 의자 위에 있습니다. 2) 나무가 창문 밖에 있습니다. / 나무는 창문 밖에 있습니다. 3) 제 친구가 방에 있습니다. / 제 친구는 방에 있습니다. 4) 가방은 옷장 안에 있습니다. / 가방이 옷장 안에 있습니다. 5) 고양이가 책 오른쪽에 있습니다. / 고양이는 책 오른쪽에 있습니다. 6) 제가 식탁 앞에 있습니다. / 저는 식탁 앞에 있습니다. 7) 일본이 한국 옆에 있습니다. / 일본은 한국 옆에 있습니다. 8) 충전기가 펜 왼쪽에 있습니다. / 충전기는 펜 왼쪽

에 있습니다.

⟨p. 78⟩
Execise 5
1) 저는 시간이 있습니다. 2) 저는 컴퓨터가 있습니다. 3) 친구는 책이 있습니다. 4) 선생님은 만화책이 없습니다. 5) 저는 돈이 없습니다. 6) 아버지가 휴대폰이 있습니까?

⟨p. 80⟩
Execise 1
1) 저는 일본에 갑니다. 2) 제 친구는 학교에 갑니다. 3) 김 교수님은 이태리에 갑니다. 4) 제 동생은 집에 갑니다. 5) 제 친구는 학교에 다닙니다. 6) 가수는 서울에 갑니다.

Exercise 2
1) 책은 테이블 아래(/밑)에 있습니다. 2) 친구는 집에 있습니다. 3) 집은 시장 오른쪽에 있습니다. 4) 시장은 건물 왼쪽에 있습니다. 5) 학교는 시장 옆에 있습니다. 6) 도시는 산 뒤에 있습니다.

Unit 8
⟨p. 83⟩
Execise 1
1) 값을 2) 몫을 3) 친구를 4) 돈을 5) 나무를 6) 돌을 7) 쌀을 8) 집을 9) 사랑을 10) 도서관을

⟨p. 86⟩
Execise 2
1) 개 두 마리 /개 2마리 2) 세(석) 잔 /3잔 3) 종이 다섯 장 / 종이 5장 4) 컴퓨터 열 대 / 컴퓨터 10대 5) 집 열두 채 / 집 12채 6) 의자 열다섯 개 / 의자 15개 7) 두 조각 / 2조각 8) 신발 여섯 켤레 / 신발 6켤레

⟨p. 89⟩
Execise 3
1) 열두시 삼십분 / 열두시 반 2) 여섯시 삼십분 / 여섯시 반 3) 저녁 아홉시 삼십분 / 아홉시 반 4) 세시 십이분 5) 일곱시 이십분 6) 다섯시 십분 7) 밤 열시 십이분 8) 저녁 일곱시 삼십오분 9) 새벽

한시 십이분 10) 오후 세시 이십삼분

Exercise 4
1) 공이에 일오팔팔에 공공오오 2) 공이에 오오삼이에 사사이일 3) 공이에 삼사오오에 이구구구 4) 공일공에 오이이에 사오팔팔 5) 공일공에 삼삼삼에 사오팔칠 6) 공일공에 팔칠오에 이사일이

⟨p. 90⟩
Exercise 5
1) 이십육 2) 사백육십팔 3) 천삼백육십구 4) 칠만 천이백삼십사 5) 사십육만 팔천사백십일 6) 백이십 사만 오천백삼십육

⟨p. 93⟩
Exercise 6
1) 1999년 4월 15일 / 천구백구십구년 사월 십오일 2) 1422년 6월 12일 / 천사백이십이년 유월 십이일 3) 1894년 10월 29일 / 천팔백구십사년 시월 이십구일 4) 2016년 6월 5일 / 이천십육년 유월 오일 5) 2003년 11월 30일 / 이천삼년 십일월 삼십일 6) 2001년 9월 11일 / 이천일년 구월 십일일

Exercise 7
1) 세시부터 네시까지 2) 그저께부터 내일까지 3) 작년부터 올해까지 4) 금요일부터 일요일까지

⟨p. 94⟩
Execise 1
1) 저는 만화책 한 권을 읽습니다. 2) 저는 햄버거를 한 개 먹습니다. 3) 저는 한국어를 공부합니다. 4) 저는 컴퓨터 한 대를 삽니다. 5) 저는 친구를 한 명 만납니다. 6) 저는 불을 켭니다.

Exercise 2
1) 1999년 4월 12일 / 천구백구십구년 사월 십이일 2) 백사십오 3) 2014년 5월 16일 / 이천십사년 오월 십육일 4) 천사백오십칠 5) 2016년 10월 20일 / 이천십육년 시월 이십일 6) 이만 삼천 사백육십육

Exercise 3
1) 아침 여덟시 삼십분 / 아침 여덟시 반 2) 오후

세시 삼십사분 3) 아침 아홉시 오분 / 오전 아홉시 오분 4) 저녁 일곱시 십이분 5) 오전 열한시 십분 6) 저녁 아홉시 십이분

Unit 9

⟨p. 97⟩
Exercise 1
1) 친구도 2) 집도 3) 일본에도 4) 중국에도 5) 선생님도 6) 나무도

Exercise 2
1) 저는 텔레비전도 봅니다. 2) 저는 집에도 갑니다. 3) 저도 (잠을) 잡니다. 4) 내 친구도 중국 사람입니다. 5) 저도 친구도 책을 읽습니다.

⟨p. 99⟩
Execise 3
1) 몰아요 2) 물어요 3) 놀아요 4) 팔아요 5) 긁어요 6) 걸어요 7) 멀어요 8) 갈아요 9) 밀어요 10) 불어요

Exercise 4
1) 써요 2) 예뻐요 3) 떠요 4) 가빠요 5) 쳐요 6) 가려요 7) 빨아요 8) 삐어요 9) 꺼요 10) 움켜줘요 11) 삼켜요 12) 벌어요 13) 봬요 14) 쩌요 15) 져요 16) 이겨요 17) 내요 18) 갈아요 19) 쏴요 20) 보여요 21) 띄어요 22) 세요 23) 아파요 24) 피어요 25) 나빠요 26) 퐈요 27) 좋아요 28) 베요 29) 꿰어요 30) 춰요

⟨p. 102⟩
Exercise 5
1) 시끄러워요 2) 귀여워요 3) 매워요 4) 미워요 5) 매끄러워요 6) 더워요 7) 가까워요 8) 씹어요 9) 고와요 10) 좁아요 11) 아쉬워요 12) 추워요 13) 구워요 14) 고아요 15) 뽑아요

⟨p. 104⟩
Exercise 1
1) 저는 만화책도 읽어요. 2) 가수는 햄버거도 먹어요 3) 저는 한국어도 공부해요. 4) 제 친구는 컴퓨터도 사요. 5) 저도 집에 가요. 6) 저도 불을 켜요.

Exercise 2
1) 아파요 2) 모여요 3) 구워요 4) 채워요 5) 익혀요 6) 매워요

Exercise 3
모자를 써요. 안경을 껴요(/써요). 장갑을 껴요. 바지를 입어요. 양말을 신어요.

Unit 10

⟨p. 107⟩
Exercise 1
1) 나는 여동생(/언니, 누나)에게 화분을 줘요. 2) 나는 이탈리아 친구에게 이메일을 보내요. 3)친구가 나에게 양말을 줘요. 4) 오빠가 여동생(/언니, 누나)에게 책을 줘요.

⟨p. 110⟩
Exercise 2
1) 개하고 고양이 2) 어제하고 오늘 3) 앞하고 뒤 4) 어머니하고 아버지 (엄마하고 아빠) 5) 나하고 말 6) 한국인하고 중국인 (한국 사람하고 중국 사람)

Exercise 3
1) 저는 책하고 신문을 읽어요. 2) 저는 학교하고 약국에 가요. 3) 그 사람은 나하고 내 친구에게 선물을 줘요. 4) 나하고 함께 가는 게 어때요?

⟨p. 112⟩
Exercise 1
1) 그 사람은 가수에게 책을 줘요. 2) 저는 (남)동생에게 사과를 줘요. 3) 저는 친구에게 이메일을 보내요. 4) 의사가 나에게 의자를 줘요. 5) 중국 친구가 나에게 휴대폰을 줘요. 6) 내 남자친구가 나에게 꽃을 줘요.

Exercise 2
1) 컴퓨터와 마우스 2) 어제와 오늘 3) 모자와 안경 4) 서울과 부산 5) 뉴욕과 시카고 6) 이탈리아와 브라질

Exercise 3

1) 나는 밥을 좋아합니다. 2) 나는 친구에게 선물을 줘요. 3) 나는 피자하고 사과를 먹어요. 4) 어머니가(/는) 우리에게 돈을 보내요. 5) 이 친구는 일본 사람이 아닙니다. 6) 나는 책을 읽어요.

Unit 11

〈p. 116〉
Exercise 1

1) 그는 한국에서 와요. 2) 선생님은 중국에서 도착해요. 3) 제 친구와 저는 식당에서 점심을 먹어요. 4) 내 일본 친구는 서울에서 일해요. 5) 저는 친구와 거실에서 이야기해요. 6) 그 작가는 한국에서 살아요.

〈p. 122〉
Exercise 1

1) 저는 서울에 살아요. 2) 저는 제 방에서 사과를 먹어요. 3) 저는 집에서 한국어를 공부해요. 4) 저는 친구 집에서 자요. 5) 저는 도서관에서 친구를 만나요. 6) 저는 거실에서 만화책을 읽어요.

Exercise 2

1) 저는 매우 피곤해요. 2) 저는 매우 슬퍼요. 3) 저는 숙제를 많이 해요. 4) 그 책은 정말 좋아요. 5) 저는 많이 말해요. / 저는 말을 많이 해요. 6) 날씨가 많이 추워요.

Exercise 3

1) 많아요 2) 괜찮아요 3) 하얘요 4) 빨라요 5) 치러요 6) 예뻐요 7) 아파요 8) 같아요 9) 옳아요

Unit 12

〈p. 125〉
Exercise 1

1) 씻어요 2) 그어요 3) 저어요 4) 이어요

〈p. 127〉
1) 저는 기차로 학교에 가요. 2) 저는 중국어로 말해요. 3) 저는 일본으로 떠나요. 4) 친구는 연필로 써요.

〈p. 129〉
1) 보세요 2) 치세요 3) 도세요 4) 노세요 5) 들으세요 6) 갚으세요 7) 벗으세요 8) 닫으세요 9) 하세요 10) 놓으세요

〈p. 130〉
Exercise 1

1) 오십니다 / 가십니다 2) 주십니다 / 만드십니다 3) 갚으십니다 / 읽으십니다 4) 닫으십니다 / 들으십니다 5) 치십니다 / 가리십니다 6) 많으십니다 / 보십니다

Exercise 2

1) 떠나세요 / 빼세요 2) 받으세요 / 주세요 3) 덮으세요 / 밟으세요 4) 좁으세요 / 추우세요 5) 웃으세요 / 나으세요 6) 도우세요 / 더우세요

Exercise 3

1) 연필로 2) 휴대폰으로 3) 비행기로 4) 돈으로 5) 불로 6) 자전거로

Unit 13

〈p. 133〉
Exercise 1

1) 저는 학교에 안 가요. 2) 저는 빵을 안 먹어요. 3) 친구는 일본으로 안 떠나요. 4) 저는 집에 안 가요. 5) 교수님은 책을 안 읽으세요. 6) 선생님은 음악을 안 들으세요. 7) 오늘 우리 집에 안 와요? 8) 도서관에서 공부를 안 해요?

〈p. 134〉
Exercise 2

1) 저는 학교에 못 가요. 2) 저는 빵을 못 먹어요. 3) 그녀의 친구는 못 떠나요. 4) 그는 요리를 못해요. 5) 오늘 내 집으로 올 수 없어요? 6) 프랑스 말을 못해요?

〈p. 135〉
Exercise 3

1) 교수님, 거기 계세요? 2) 선생님, 펜이 있으세요? 3) 할머니는 식당에 계세요. 4) 할아버지는 병원에 계세요.

⟨p. 138⟩
Exercise 1
1) 저는 언니(/누나, 여동생)한테서 책을 받아요.
2) 저는 교수님에게서 편지를 받아요. 3) 그 사람
은 친구에게서 이메일을 받아요. 4) 그녀는 엄마에
게서 선물을 받아요. 5) 교수님은 학생에게서 편지
를 받아요.

Exercise 2
1) 어머니는 신문을 읽으십니다. 2) 할머니는 잘
드십니다/잡수십니다. 3) 아버지는 집에서 주무
십니다. 4) 할아버지는 편찮으십니다. 5) 아버지
는 조용히 말씀하십니다. 6) 김 선생님은 도서관
에 가십니다.

Exercise 3
교수님, 성함이 어떻게 되세요? 이름은 김은정이
에요. 어느 나라 사람이에요? 프랑스사람이에요.
언제까지 이탈리아에 계세요? 내년까지 있어요.
감사합니다.

Unit 14
⟨p. 141⟩
Execise 1
1) 선생님께서 저에게 펜을 주십니다. 2)저는 아
버지께 신문을 드립니다. 3) 제 아버지는 저에게
10,000원을 줍니다. 4) 저는 사장님께 말씀드립
니다.

⟨p. 142⟩
Exercise 2
1) 선생님께서 연구실에서 주무십니다. 2) 선생님
께서도 중국으로 떠나십니다. 3) 저는 할머니께 가방
을 드립니다. 4)선생님께서는 컴퓨터가 있으십니다.

⟨p. 143⟩
Execise 3
1) 드십시오 2) 치십시오 3) 주무십시오 4) 주십
시오 5) 물으십시오 6) 도십시오 7) 닫으십시오 8)
입으십시오 9) 사십시오 10) 하십시오

⟨p. 144⟩
Exercise 4
1) 먹었습니다 2) 피었습니다 3) 잤습니다 4) 주었
습니다/줬습니다 5) 물었습니다/묻었습니다 6) 돌
았습니다 7) 닫았습니다 8) 입었습니다 9) 그랬습
니다 10) 했습니다

Exercise 5
1) 선생님께서 돌아가셨습니다. 2) 어제 선생님
께서 대학교에 안 오셨습니다. 3) 교수님께서 많
이 드셨습니다. 4) 사장님께서 책 두 권을 주셨습
니다.

⟨p. 145⟩
Exercise 6
1) 바나나랑 딸기 2) 수박이랑 귤 3) 멜론이랑 레
몬 4) 포도랑 복숭아

⟨p. 146⟩
Exercise 1
1) 선생님께서는 2) 교수님께서 3) 교수님께 4) 선
생님께 5) 할머니께서 6) 사장님께

Exercise 2
1) 교수님께서 서울에 가십니다. 2) 내일 그의 아
버지께서도 오십니다. 3) 사장님께서 우리에게 선
물을 주십니다. 4) 작가하고 교수님께서 점심을 드
십니다. 5) 할아버지께서 집에 안 계십니다. 6) 할
아버지께서 물을 드십니다.

Exercise 3
1) 가셨어요 2) 보셨어요 3) 주셨어요 4) 드셨어
요/잡수셨어요 5) 돌아가셨어요 6) 주무셨어요

ESSENTIAL BIBLIOGRAPHY

Ahn Junmyeong, *Korean Grammar in Use*, Darakwon, Seoul, 2010.

Bruno A.L. - Ahn Miran, *Corso di lingua coreana*, HOEPLI, Milano, 2009.

Byon Andrew Sangpil, *Basic Korean (A grammar and workbook)*, Routledge, New York, 2009.

De Benedittis A. - Kim Huntae, *I caratteri cinesi nella lingua coreana*, HOEPLI, Milano, 2013.

Kim-Renaud Y.K., *Korean: an Essential Grammar*, Routledge, New York, 2009.

Kim-Renaud Y.K.,*The Korean Alphabet (Its History and Structure)*, University of Hawai'i Press, Honolulu, 1997.

King R. - Yeon Jaehun, *Elementary Korean*, Tuttle Publishing, North Clarendon, 2009.

Riotto M., *Introduzione allo studio della lingua coreana*, Istituto Universitario Orientale, Napoli, 1990.

Seoul National University Eoneo gyoyugweon, *Woegugin-eull wi-han Han*gugeo *bareum 47*, vv.1-2, Korea Language Plus, Seoul, 2009.

Yi Huija - Yi Chonghui, *Eomi-josa hakseupja-yong sajeon*, Hanguk Munhwasa, Seoul, 2006.

Credits

Author	Andrea De Benedittis
Publisher	Kim Hyunggeun
Editor	Park Minseo
Copy Editor	Eileen Cahill
Designer	Cynthia Fernandez
Graphic Project	Andrea De Benedittis
Illustrations	Luigino Colabrodo
English Translation	Andrea De Benedittis, Carla Vitantonio
Proofreading	Thomas Connor Bahlo
Speaker	Lee Sang Suk
Audio registration and postproduction	Mario Santinello / True Colours Studio